CW00921083

DRAMA CLASSIC COLLECTIONS

These volumes collect together the most popular plays from a single author or a particular period. Both affordable and accessible, they offer students, actors and theatregoers a series of uncluttered texts in impeccable editions, accompanied by comprehensive introductions. Where the originals are in English, there is an end-glossary of unfamiliar words and phrases. Where the originals are in a foreign language, the translations aim to be both actable and accurate – and are made by translators whose work is regularly staged in the professional theatre.

Other Drama Classic Collections

CHEKHOV – FOUR PLAYS

The Seagull
Uncle Vanya
Three Sisters
The Cherry Orchard

IBSEN – THREE PLAYS

A Doll's House
Ghosts
Hedda Gabler

GREEK TRAGEDY

Antigone
Bacchae
Medea

RESTORATION COMEDY

The Country Wife
The Rover
The Way of the World

WILDE – FOUR PLAYS

Lady Windermere's Fan
A Woman of No Importamce
An Ideal Husband
The Importance of Being Earnest

LORCA

Blood Wedding
Yerma
The House of Bernarda Alba

translated and introduced by
JO CLIFFORD

NICK HERN BOOKS
London
www.nickhern....o.uk

A Drama Classic

This collection first published in Great Britain in 2017 as a paperback original by Nick Hern Books Limited, The Glasshouse, 49a Goldhawk Road, London W12 8QP

Typeset by Country Setting, Kingsdown, Kent CT14 8ES
Printed in Great Britain by Mimeo Ltd, Huntingdon, Cambridgeshire PE29 6XX

A CIP catalogue record for this book is available from the British Library

ISBN 978 1 84842 632 0

Contents

Key Dates

1898   5 June, Federico García Lorca born in Fuente Vaqueros, near Granada, Spain.

1909   His family move to Granada.

1914   Lorca enters Granada University to study law, on his father's insistence. Lorca had wanted to study music.

1919   Lorca enters the Residencia de Estudiantes in Madrid.

1920   22 March, Lorca's first play, *The Butterfly's Evil Spell*, opens in Madrid. It is a catastrophic failure.

1921   Publication of Lorca's first book of poems, *Libro de poemas*.

1922   The painter, Salvador Dali, then eighteen, arrives in Madrid. He and Lorca become close friends.

1924–5 Lorca completes two more plays: *Mariana Pineda* and *The Shoemaker's Amazing Wife*.

1927   *Mariana Pineda* finally produced. It is an astonishing success.

1928   Publication of *Gypsy Ballads*.

1929   *The Love of Don Perlimplin* is about to be produced in Madrid, but the theatre is closed by the dictatorship.

        Lorca leaves for New York, where he witnesses the Wall Street crash.

1930   Lorca returns to Spain via Cuba.

1931   Collapse of the dictatorship: establishment of the Spanish Republic.

1932   Lorca sets up La Barraca theatre company and begins touring the villages of Spain with productions of plays by Lope de Vega, Tirso de Molina and Calderón.

1933   Triumphant first production of *Blood Wedding*. Hitler's rise to power in Germany.

1933–4   Lorca visits Argentina, where his work is triumphantly received.

1934   The opening night of *Yerma* scandalises right-wing and traditional Catholic opinion.

1936   Successful opening of *Dona Rosita the Spinster.* Growing political unrest in Spain. Lorca writes *The House of Bernarda Alba.*

1936   14 July, Lorca returns to his parents in Granada.

         17 July, reads *The House of Bernarda Alba* to his friends in Granada.

         18 July, rebel right-wing uprising led by General Franco marks beginning of Civil War.

         23 July, right-wing rebels take over Granada.

         18 August, Federico García Lorca murdered by fascists.

Introduction

Federico García Lorca (1898–1936)

Lorca was born on 5 June 1898. The year was a hugely significant one in Spanish cultural and political history: it gave its name to a whole generation of writers who used the events of this year as a rallying cry in efforts to convince the Spanish people of their country's deplorable state and the desperate need for re-evaluation and change. They were called the 'Generation of '98', and they included Azorín, Baroja and Ángel Ganivet.

The historical event that inspired this movement was the disastrous war with the United States which led to the loss of Cuba, Spain's last remaining colony. This apparently distant event was to have huge repercussions for Lorca. Cuba had been Spain's principal source of sugar; Lorca's father was to be astute enough to plant his land with sugar beet, and with the aid of a series of successful land purchases, he was to become one of the richest men in the Fuente Vaqueros district.

A long-term consequence of this was that Lorca himself never needed to earn his own living. There's no question this wealthy background contributed both to the large volume, and the technical and emotional daring, of his work. As it happened, *Blood Wedding* in particular was hugely successful; but the financial security of his position left him absolutely free to write as he wanted without regard to the demands of the commercial theatre of his day.

However, the most immediate consequence for the young Lorca was that he spent his childhood as the rich son of the wealthiest landowner of a mainly poor village.

Perhaps the best way for us to imagine the impact on Lorca's sensibility is to think of our own feelings towards the desperately poor of the Third World – or the homeless that many of us pass each day on the street. The contrast between his wealth and the poverty of so many of those around him left a deep impression on Lorca, which he was to express in later life in his autobiographical essay 'My Village'.

The plight of one family affected Lorca particularly deeply. One of his friends in the village was a little girl whose father was a chronically ill day labourer and whose mother was the exhausted victim of countless pregnancies. The one day on which Federico was not allowed to visit their home was washing day: the members of this family had only one set of clothes, and they had to stay inside their house while their only clothes were being washed and dried. Lorca wrote:

> When I returned home on those occasions, I would look into the wardrobe, full of clean, fragrant clothes, and feel dreadfully anxious, with a dead weight on my heart.

He grew up with a profound sense of indignation at this kind of injustice:

> No one dares to ask for what he needs. No one dares… to demand bread. And I who say this grew up among these thwarted lives. I protest against this mistreatment of those who work the land.

The young man who wrote this protest at the end of his adolescence maintained a profound anger right to the end of his life. In an interview he gave in 1936, he stated: 'As long as there is economic injustice in the world, the world will be unable to think clearly.'

He continued the interview with a fable to illustrate the difficulties of creating valid art in a situation of economic injustice:

> Two men are walking along a riverbank. One of them is rich, the other poor. One has a full belly and the other fouls the air with his yawns. And the rich man says: 'What a lovely little boat out on the water! Look at that lily blooming on the bank!' And the poor man wails: 'I'm hungry, so hungry!' Of course. The day when hunger is eradicated there is going to be the greatest spiritual explosion the world has ever seen. I'm talking like a real socialist, aren't I?

For Lorca, the art of creating theatre was totally bound up with the process of creating a better society:

> The idea of art for art's sake is something that would be cruel if it weren't, fortunately, so ridiculous. No decent person believes any longer in all that nonsense about pure art, art for

art's sake. At this dramatic moment in time, the artist should laugh and cry with his people. We must put down the bouquet of lilies and bury ourselves up to the waist in mud to help those who are looking for lilies. For myself, I have a genuine need to communicate with others. That's why I knocked at the door of the theatre and why I now devote all my talents to it.

This passionate anger at the injustice of human society, and equally passionate determination to create art that might remedy it, were fuelled not simply by his childhood experiences. As an adult, he had travelled to New York, and witnessed at first hand the devastating impact of the Wall Street Crash:

It's the spectacle of all the world's money in all its splendour, its mad abandon and its cruelty… This is where I have got a clear idea of what a huge mass of people fighting to make money is really like. The truth is that it's an international war with just a thin veneer of courtesy… We ate breakfast on a thirty-second floor with the head of a bank, a charming person with a cold and feline side quite English. People came in there after being paid. They were all counting dollars. Their hands all had the characteristic tremble that holding money gives them… Colin [an acquaintance] had five dollars in his purse and I three. Despite this he said to me: 'We're surrounded by millions and yet the only two decent people here are you and I.'

And when he writes so angrily of the 'thwarted lives' of those whose existence is dominated by money, it is clear Lorca is thinking not simply of the plight of the rural poor, but also of the bourgeoisie to which he himself, and many of us, now belong.

He is concerned not simply with the suffering that a wealthy middle class inflicts on those beneath them on the social scale; he is equally concerned with the suffering they inflict upon themselves. The 'thwarted lives' he saw in his village are not simply those of the poor.

Lorca perceived this very clearly: for the comparative wealth possessed by the families involved in the wedding contract in *Blood Wedding* brings them no happiness. All the main characters in the play seem trapped by the conventions and the demands of the society they inhabit.

Lorca and Theatre

Lorca once said that you could judge the health of a nation's culture by looking at the state of its theatre. And for him theatre was a natural extension of poetry: a poetry that leaps off the printed page, escapes from between the pages of books 'and becomes human. It shouts and speaks. It cries and despairs'.

For Lorca there was nothing precious about poetry; it was simply part of living. He once wrote: 'Poetry is something that just walks along the street.'

Because for him it was a part of living, to be deprived of it was a kind of torment; and to deprive people of the chance of experiencing it was a kind of crime. In an interview he gave to an English journalist, he spoke of his anger at the lack of theatre that was the norm in Spain outside the capital: 'Theatre is almost dead outside Madrid, and the people suffer accordingly, as they would if they had lost eyes or ears or sense of taste.'

He also said, 'I will always be on the side of those who have nothing.' He was a political writer in the deepest sense, in that the act of writing was part of the struggle for a better world.

> Sometimes, when I think of what is going on in the world, I wonder why am I writing? The answer is that one simply has to work. Work and go on working. Work and help everyone who deserves it. Work even though at times it feels like so much wasted effort. Work as a form of protest. For one's impulse has to be to cry out every day one wakes up and is confronted by misery and injustice of every kind: I protest! I protest! I protest!

All these concerns came together in Lorca's work for La Barraca, the travelling theatre he helped to found in the early years of the Republic. They would set up a simple stage in the town square and perform the great, and then almost completely neglected, classics of the Spanish theatre – the works of Lope de Vega, Tirso de Molina and Calderón.

His work on this incredibly bold and imaginative precursor of our own small-scale touring companies had a profound effect on Lorca. Experiencing the impact these classics made on a mass audience was a source of strength and inspiration; and working on the texts themselves must surely have deepened his remarkable theatre-writing skills.

Nature and Folk Culture

Lorca paints a bleak picture of rural life in these plays. But there are moments when we catch glimpses of a very different view of the countryside. The songs that celebrate the wedding of *Blood Wedding* or the folk wisdom personified by the maid in Act Two Scene Two of the same play: these offer us glimpses of a natural world full of joyfulness, beauty and fertility.

This is actually far more like the world Lorca mostly saw as a child. The love of it always remained with him, and, as he said himself, the natural world remained a source of inspiration throughout his life:

> I love the countryside. I feel myself linked to it in all my emotions. My oldest childhood memories have the flavour of the earth. The meadows, the fields, have done wonders for me. The wild animals of the countryside, the livestock, the people living on the land, all these have a fascination very few people grasp. I recall them now exactly as I knew them in my childhood.

A still more important source of inspiration was the speech of the villagers:

> My whole childhood was centred on the village. Shepherds, fields, sky, solitude. Total simplicity. I'm often surprised when people think that the things in my work are daring improvisations of my own, a poet's audacities. Not at all. They're authentic details, and seem strange to a lot of people because it's not often that we approach life in such a simple, straightforward fashion: looking and listening. Such an easy thing, isn't it?… I have a huge storehouse of childhood recollections in which I can hear the people speaking. This is poetic memory, and I trust it implicitly.

'This is poetic memory': here we have another key to Lorca's creativity. As he said himself, he had in his memory a huge 'storehouse' of snatches of folklore, popular expressions and popular song: a storehouse he could draw on whenever necessary to produce a dazzling array of extraordinary imagery.

This is something denied to most of us, growing up in this age, this place, and this time. The industrial revolution has almost completely erased our folk heritage, and severed our connections with it. In Scotland, this process was deliberately begun by the destruction of the clan culture following the collapse of the Jacobite rebellion in 1745. In England, where I grew up, the process was less brutal but perhaps more thorough; and folk culture, if it still lives at all, is mostly preserved in museums or in those festivals in which middle-aged people rather self-consciously dress up as Morris dancers, clog dancers, or dancers round the maypole.

Because we have never known it, it is hard for us to appreciate what this folk culture meant, or even measure exactly what it is we have lost. Lorca's biographer, Ian Gibson, expresses it beautifully:

> Lorca inherited all the vigour of a speech that springs from the earth and expresses itself with extraordinary spontaneity. Indeed, one has only to hear the inhabitants of the Vega talk and observe their colourful use of imagery to realise that the metaphorical language of Lorca's theatre and poetry, which seems... so original, is rooted in an ancient, collective awareness of nature in which all things – trees, horses, mountains, the moon and the sun, rivers, flowers, human beings – are closely related and interdependent.

Those of us who live in Scotland are fortunate in that to a certain extent spoken Scots still retains some of its vivid capacity for metaphor, its sense of shared culture, its vibrant energy and sense of utter delight in the richness of the spoken word – characteristics that have been beautifully exploited in plays like Tony Roper's *The Steamie* or Liz Lochhead's *Mary Queen of Scots Got Her Head Chopped Off.*

To get a proper sense of Lorca's work, it is most important to reflect on this linguistic richness (which rarely, if ever, comes across in translation), and particularly to reflect on the way in which we all employ and enjoy the use of metaphors – 'black affronted', 'you tube', or 'a load of mince'. It is sad but necessary to add, though, that this is all pretty poor stuff compared to the immense linguistic richness Lorca had at his disposal, and which shines through all his poetry and his plays.

In a celebrated lecture Lorca gave on imagery in the work of the seventeenth-century poet Gongora, he spoke of the connections between this poet's supposedly highly artificial and obscure use of imagery and the completely spontaneous and unaffected use of imagery of the people of Andalucia. For instance, where he came from, Lorca explained, when people want to describe water flowing strongly and slowly along a deep irrigation channel they talk of the 'ox of the water' – a surprising and beautiful image that encapsulates the water's slowness, strength, and even the visual impression of the water patterns made as you wade through it. Similarly, when one of his cousins was teaching him how to boil eggs, she told him to put the eggs in the water 'when it starts to laugh'.

Gender Issues

Blood Wedding, *Yerma* and *The House of Bernarda Alba* are generally thought of as a trilogy of Lorca's plays portraying the repression of women in Spanish rural life. In each play, Lorca portrays a world whose sexual mores trap women in an odiously repressive set of double standards that expect men to give full rein to their sexuality but savagely punish any woman who expresses hers. The central characters of these three plays, on the contrary, are all women whose sexuality is denied them, women trapped in a repressive society which denies them the possibility of life itself.

If we are to understand this fully, we must again try to put it into the context of Lorca's own life and experience. By all accounts he was in some respects a very solitary child. Long periods of ill health kept him in isolation from other children; and besides he suffered from a slight deformity. He had extremely flat feet, and one leg was slightly shorter than the other which meant he walked with a very characteristic sway.

Like many a lonely child, he took refuge in the richness of his imagination; something all the more important to him as he grew older and attended secondary school where he was bullied and ridiculed by some of his more brutal classmates. They said he was effeminate and gave him the nickname of 'Federica'.

As he grew older, his inner isolation was deepened by the realisation of his homosexuality; and this led to a profound inner anguish which it is important we make the imaginative effort to understand.

The machismo of Spanish culture has been traditionally associated with a deep loathing of homosexuality which has only recently begun to dissipate. Even as recently as 1971, I remember a male friend in Granada telling me that, 'To be homosexual is the greatest misfortune that can befall a man.'

In the far more traditional Spain of the twenties and thirties, Lorca's sexuality was a source of profound shame, a secret he of necessity had to conceal from his parents and from everyone except his most intimate friends.

It is important to take a moment to reflect on what this means: not as an abstraction, but as an experience lived through in the imagination. It means that when he felt attracted to someone, he was not able to reach out and touch them; not able to express tenderness or affection; not able to put his arm round someone in the street, not able to kiss them. It means feeling obliged to deny the deepest impulses of body and heart: obliged both to deny and to repress them. It means every sexual encounter has to happen in secret and runs the risk of exposure and betrayal. In short, it means being denied the most fundamental of human freedoms. And these are the very same freedoms denied the women in this play.

So in these plays Lorca is making a statement about the situation of women suffering repression; and it is also important we find the connections between their situation and that of the homosexual suffering repression in a homophobic society. And perhaps we also need to reflect on the way boys in general are brought up in our own culture and our own time: in the denial of spontaneity and the denial of tenderness. For in the end, the forces that repress women repress the whole of humanity.

Blood Wedding

What Happens in the Play

Act One Scene One   The bridegroom asks his mother for a knife. He is going to his vineyard, and he wants to cut grapes. This frightens her, and brings up her grief at the loss of her husband and other son. They were killed by knives in a feud with another family of the village, the Felix. The young man wants his mother to leave her grief be; he wants her to consent to his proposed marriage. She agrees to buy the betrothal gifts, and make the visit to the bride-to-be's family as custom demands. After her son's departure, a neighbour enters. The mother discovers from her that the girl used to have a relationship with a young man, which got broken off, and that the young man, Leonardo, belonged to the clan of the Felix. The scene ends on a note of foreboding.

Act One Scene Two   A young mother sings a lullaby to her baby. We learn the baby's father is Leonardo; that his marriage is an unhappy one; and that there are rumours that he is riding over to see his former lover. The scene ends with the lullaby, which has now also been tainted with foreboding.

Act One Scene Three   The mother and her son have come to visit the bride-to-be and her father. The father welcomes the proposed marriage, because he sees it as furthering his commercial interests. The bride-to-be is, however, in two minds about her proposed marriage. And at the very end of the act, it becomes clear that Leonardo is riding over to see her.

Act Two Scene One   The bride-to-be is getting dressed for her wedding. We learn she is herself the daughter of an unhappy marriage. Leonardo has ridden ahead of the other guests to arrive first; the bride-to-be breaks all the conventions by seeing him. We learn that they still desire each other; that their proposed marriage was broken off because he was considered too poor; and that the bride-to-be is getting married now to try to still the passion that continues to consume her. The songs of the guests to celebrate the coming wedding strike a deeply ironic note.

Act Two Scene Two   It is some hours later, and the maid is happily preparing the wedding meal for when everyone returns from the church. The father remains complacent about the wedding, and the prospect of grandchildren to work his land; the mother wrestles with her forebodings; the bride-to-be remains mired in her inner conflict.

The bridegroom does his poor best to be correct. It gradually becomes clear that Leonardo and the bride-to-be have eloped together. The bridegroom and his mother gather the guests together to set off to pursue them and get revenge.

Act Three Scene One   We are in a wood at night. Three wood-cutters, who gradually seem to us to represent elemental forces of nature, tell of the couple's flight and the noose tightening around them. The moon enters, personified by another woodcutter: a sinister figure, hungry for the couple's blood. Death enters, personified by an old beggarwoman. The moon will shed his eerie light on the fleeing couple to ensure they are seen and caught by their pursuers. The bridegroom stumbles over Death. She promises to guide him to his prey. The pursued couple enter, still in the grip of a passion they know to be self-destructive, but which they also know they cannot deny. Soon after they leave, we hear two piercing screams; Death opens her cloak like a black bird with outspread wings. The curtain descends in deep silence.

Final Scene   Young girls are spinning thread. Leonardo's wife and mother enter in deep mourning. Then the bridegroom's mother, and her neighbour from the first act. We understand that the bridegroom and Leonardo have killed each other. The bride enters to expose herself to the mother's rage. She hopes she will kill her, but the older woman discovers she cannot. The play ends on a note of suffering without respite or hope.

Sources

A few months after *Blood Wedding* opened in 1933, Lorca gave an interview in which he declared that the original idea for it came from a press report he had read about a murder that took place in Almería.

Recently discovered press reports confirm that this was in fact the case. A young bride eloped with her cousin just after her wedding the couple had been pursued by outraged relatives and the young man had been killed.

In perhaps less direct ways, too, we can see that Lorca drew inspiration in this play, as in all his others, from the events and social structures that shaped his own life.

Blood Wedding on Stage

The play opened in the Teatro Beatriz in Madrid on 8 March 1933. Since the moment of its opening, it has had continuous commercial success. The first production ran for two months in Madrid, another two months in Barcelona; the play was then produced in Buenos Aires, where it ran for more than a hundred performances. The triumphant success of this production, supervised by Lorca himself, was the precursor to equally successful transfers back to Madrid and Barcelona in 1935.

It was published in 1936, translated into French and English that same year; and since then has been repeatedly staged throughout Europe and the Americas, where it is universally recognised as one of the major plays of the twentieth century.

A major literary source for the play were the plays of Synge, which Lorca read in translation while at the Residencia de Estudiantes; perhaps that is one reason why the play has been translated and performed so often in Ireland, where the action of the play is often relocated to the Irish countryside.

In a way, the play's continuing popularity and success is surprising, given the difficulties involved in staging it well. In the West, it is extraordinarily hard to create a convincing stage picture of a society so profoundly connected with the earth to an audience so profoundly alienated from it.

Also, given the profound transformation in the situation of women in the West, it may be tempting to dismiss the play on the grounds that 'such things don't happen any more'.

Perhaps it is worth remembering that the majority of women in the contemporary world still live under conditions of patriarchy as oppressive as those Lorca describes; or that a recent survey by the United Nations estimates that there are more casualties resulting from acts of violence against women than from all current conventional wars.

Lorca's profound compassion for suffering humanity and his passionate protest on behalf of those suffering oppression of all kinds need to be heard more than ever.

Yerma

What Happens in the Play

Act One Scene One   Yerma is dreaming. Someone is singing a lullaby: a shepherd leads a child to her by the hand.

She wakes to the childless reality of the real morning. Her husband Juan is going out to work in the fields. It quickly becomes clear that her desire for a child is at odds with his desire for money. He leaves her in sadness.

Maria, a young woman who has recently got married, comes in, full of excitement. She has just discovered she is pregnant. Her joy deepens Yerma's sense of longing.

Yerma has agreed to sew some baby clothes for Maria. When Victor enters and sees her sewing, he assumes it is because she has become pregnant, and congratulates her. We understand from the way they are together that they have desired each other for many years, and have been forced to repress this desire.

Act One Scene Two   Yerma is on her way back from taking her husband his food in the fields. The first person she meets is an old woman totally in touch with the earth. Yerma asks her for advice. The old woman asks if there is real desire between her and her husband. It becomes clear Yerma has married – and remains with – her husband out of duty.

The old woman seems to sense the hopelessness of Yerma's position and leaves her without giving the advice Yerma asks for. Then Yerma meets two young women. One has left her baby alone in the house; Yerma instils her with fear for her child's welfare.

The other is a rebel who is glad not to have children and utterly rejects the traditional values Yerma so unquestioningly follows.

Then she encounters Victor, and is profoundly moved by his song. Profound erotic currents rise to the surface as they speak; but Juan's arrival interrupts them.

Juan tells Yerma he is spending the night in the fields because it is his turn to receive the water for irrigation. His farm is clearly more important to him than she is, and the act ends with her left alone, rejected and angry.

Act Two Scene One   The village women have been washing their clothes in a stream. They are a kind of Chorus whose individual voices comment on Yerma's situation and judge her in it.

We learn her behaviour is beginning to cause scandal in the village and that Juan has brought in his two sisters to watch over her.

Gossip is cut short by the arrival of the two women themselves. The flocks of sheep are being gathered together: they are like an army. But one person's flock is missing: Victor's.

The women break into a lyrical song of motherhood, and the joy a new child can bring into the world.

Act Two Scene Two   Juan is at home with his two sisters. Yerma is out getting water. Juan is angry that his sisters have let her out; he wants her kept in. When Yerma returns home, he reproaches her for her continuing unhappiness. She reproaches him, even if indirectly, for their lack of children. He goes in to eat; she remains on stage, and lyrically expresses her longing for fulfilment as a wife and a mother.

Maria comes in with her child. Yerma holds him; sees he has the same eyes as his mother, and weeps.

The rebellious young woman of the first act comes in to tell Yerma that her mother, the local wise woman and witch, is ready to take her to the graveyard tonight to perform a magic ceremony that will give her a child.

Victor enters. He and his family are leaving the village, and he has come in to bid Juan and Yerma farewell. Juan has bought Victor's herd; Juan's affairs are prospering, but his and Yerma's emotional life is clearly sterile.

When the two men have gone, Yerma slips out with the young woman to go to the house of her mother the witch.

Juan's two sisters come onto the stage in the gathering darkness to look for her. As they call after her, for the first time we hear her name spoken out loud: Yerma!

It is crucial the audience understand what the name means: barren, sterile – a word for wasteland.

Act Three Scene One   Yerma is in the house of Dolores, the witch, after performing the fertility ritual in the graveyard. Dolores is impressed by the courage Yerma has shown, tells her the ritualistic prayers she must repeat, and assures her she will have a child.

Yerma is desperate: aware of the frigidity of her husband, but trapped by the demands of her conventional values. Dawn is beginning to break, but it's as if she cannot bear to return to her emotionally cold home.

Juan and his sisters burst into the house, having been out looking for her. Juan, too, is desperate. The situation is becoming intolerable for him. Yerma fiercely defends her integrity and faithfulness. She tries to come close to him, but he rejects her. She curses him at the top of her voice. Juan insists she keeps quiet to maintain decorum. She seems to submit and quietly returns with him to their house, which for her is now a prison.

Final Scene   Women are gathering for a pilgrimage to the shrine of a supposedly miracle-working saint, whose effigy apparently has the powers to make women fertile. Among them is the pagan old woman of the first act, who takes the rather more cynical, if realistic, view that the whole pilgrimage also attracts men and provides the opportunity for sexual encounters between them and the women. It's this that makes the women fertile; and it's this that is strongly suggested by the explicit dance between two masked figures representing the male and the female.

Yerma encounters the old woman, who tells her very plainly that it's her husband who is to blame for her infertility, and offers her the chance to go with her son instead. Yerma refuses. She is still bound by the demands of her honour, and the old woman loses all sympathy for her and abandons her to her fate.

It turns out Juan has been listening. Their utter incompatibility becomes brutally clear. He tells her he does not ever want a child, but he wants to be reconciled to her. He asks her to kiss him: in her fury and disgust, Yerma kills him. She shouts out to the other pilgrims that she has killed her husband, and she has also killed her hopes of a child.

Title

'Yerma' is a proper name that Lorca invented. He created it through giving the feminine ending to the Spanish word *'yermo'*, which is a word which describes wasteland, barren ground, land without cultivation, land which can never bear harvest or fruit.

Lorca took great care not to have anyone address Yerma directly by name until the end of Act Two in order to give it the strongest possible dramatic impact. Particularly because Yerma is not actually a woman's name, the first audiences would have been acutely aware of its meaning and its power. Which is why it is particularly important that an English-speaking audience doesn't just respond to the word as if it were a woman's name without understanding its meaning and significance. For that reason I have not followed the usual practice of leaving the word untranslated in the title. The audience needs to understand it. This is all the more important because, far more than in any other Lorca play, Yerma herself is the absolute centre of the play. Even on those rare occasions she is physically absent from the stage, she and her situation are always the central focus of the dialogue.

It is significant that, in his subtitle, Lorca does not describe *Yerma* as a play. Instead he calls it: 'A Tragic Poem in Three Acts and Six Scenes'. And one could argue that it barely functions as a play at all. There is an absolute minimum of plot. There is little, if any, character development. What we have instead is an isolated individual in an appalling situation from which she is both unwilling and unable to escape. The noose slowly tightens about her, until in the end she condemns herself to the utter sterility that has, in effect, been hers since the very beginning. In fact in all kinds of ways it shouldn't work as a play at all. The fact that it does work has, I think, to be due to the extraordinary intensity of Lorca's writing and his total empathy with his protagonist.

Sources

In his very touching memoir of his brother, Francisco García Lorca describes how their father used to keep a portrait of his childless first wife, Matilde Palacios, in their childhood home.

Lorca himself wrote that his childhood was 'an obsession with certain silver place settings and with portraits of the woman who might have been my mother'. He also mentions the annual pilgrimage to Moclín, where every year there was a procession of childless women to the little hermitage on the hill where the 'True Effigy of the Most Holy Christ of the Cloth' was claimed to grant the miraculous gift of fertility to the childless.

There was a lithograph of the effigy in their country house which Lorca used to contemplate and remark upon. And every year the procession would pass through their village on the way to the shrine, greeted by the derisive shouts of 'Cuckolds!' – aimed at the husbands of the childless women – that grew from the rumours about the rather more down-to-earth explanation of the miracle.

In perhaps less direct ways, too, we can see that Lorca drew inspiration in this play, as in all his others, from the events and social structures that shaped his own life.

Yerma on Stage

The play opened in the Teatro Español in Madrid on 29 December 1934.

It was a highly charged political event. Both the dress rehearsal and the opening night were attended by many prominent literary and political figures of the left, together with hecklers from the right, who hurled homophobic insults at both Lorca and his leading actress, Margarita Xirgu. The great film director Luis Buñuel was also present, in agony from sciatica. The days of his association with Lorca were long over; true to form, he hated the play and walked, or rather limped, out at the end of the first scene of Act Two. The audience, and critics of the left, all adored it. The play was a huge commercial success and ran for more than 130 performances. The right-wing press, however, loathed it, and it became the focus of vicious attacks. It cemented Lorca's reputation among the right as a left-wing homosexual degenerate and in that sense contributed to the hatred that led to his assassination.

When it opened in Barcelona a few months later, it became the focus of Catalan nationalism. It is curious how so apparently apolitical a play should become the focus of such intense political passions – and continued to be so long after Lorca's death.

From 1939 onwards, the fascist dictatorship that governed Spain after the Civil War did everything it could to suppress Lorca's writing. Performance of his plays was not permitted for many years, though *Yerma* was the first play to break through the barrier of censorship. After immense difficulties, this performance took place in the Teatro Eslava in Madrid in autumn 1960. It was only allowed on condition there was no publicity, and the theatre was surrounded by armed police. Aurora Bautista, the actress in the leading role, still remained profoundly moved by the emotions of that first night in an interview she gave twenty-four years later, in 1984: 'It was so profoundly moving… the first performance of a work by Lorca since the end of the Civil War… At the end, a basket of red flowers was left on the stage and everyone shouted: "Federico! Federico!" '

Another justly celebrated production was that directed by Victor García in 1971 and performed by Núria Espert. The production dispensed with the realistic settings specified in the text. Instead, it was all performed on something resembling a gigantic spider's web that could transform into all the settings the play demands, and which embodied the entrapment of the central character.

I was fortunate enough to see its revival in Edinburgh in 1986 on the night of the fiftieth anniversary of Federico's murder. It changed my artistic life for ever.

Looking back, I understand it was because it enabled me to see how it was possible to create theatre that is unashamedly emotional and absolutely not tied to being literally representational.

This is a kind of theatre that remains quite alien to the British tradition. Reading Michael Billington's *Guardian* review of the production of the play at the National Theatre the following year, with its 'tasteful gypsy dancing accompanied by a decorous trio on guitar and violin' makes one understand just how much the play is wonderfully un-English.

It is undeniably a real gift for the right female actor; probably the most successful English-speaking production has been Helena Kaut-Howson's staging at London's Arcola Theatre in 2006 with Kathryn Hunter in the title role.

It remains an extraordinarily demanding play to stage, and perhaps it is tempting to dismiss it as outdated.

But it is worth remembering that the majority of women in the contemporary world still live under conditions of patriarchy as oppressive as those Lorca describes; and so it remains, very defiantly, a fierce act of resistance. Lorca's profound compassion for humanity and his passionate protest on behalf of those suffering oppression of all kinds need to be heard more than ever.

Translator's Thanks

Thanks are due to Thomas Bailey, Thomas Wells and Alex Haigh, who insisted I finish this translation in time for their production in the Donald Roy Theatre, University of Hull, in February 2009. The following cast and production members also helped me to revise it: Busola Afolabi, Aimee Brehany, Ailsa Campbell, Kelly-Anne Chambers, Hannah Charter, Katie Driver, Emma Filby, Laura Fletcher, Sarah Gosnell, Jodie Howard, Joel Keating, Sam Kenny, Jess Pendlebury, Joel Redgrave, Rosie Tinker, Katie Waller, Kimberley Waller, Harriet Warnock, Sarah Williams and Hannah Wood.

The House of Bernarda Alba

What Happens in the Play

Act One   Offstage, the bells are tolling for Bernarda's second husband's funeral. La Poncia, Bernarda's housekeeper, is eating a sausage she stole from the larder. The (unnamed) maid is scrubbing the floor. Both share a common hatred for Bernarda, who is tight-fisted and domineering. La Poncia has been working for her for thirty years, and dreams of the humiliations she would like to inflict on her in revenge. A major anxiety for both is that the house be spotlessly clean; and that Bernarda's mad mother, María Josefa, stay safely under lock and key.

La Poncia leaves to catch the last responses in church; the maid brutally repulses a hungry beggar woman, continues cleaning, cursing the dead man as she does so. It's the last time he'll molest her behind the stable door.

As Bernarda enters, she bursts into passionate weeping. The whole stage fills with women in black. In the midst of pious conversation, they gossip viciously behind Bernarda's back. Bernarda curses the women after they have gone. She lays down the law to her daughters: mourning will last for eight years. Eight years of utter seclusion.

But there is an immediate threat to her control: the eldest daughter, Angustias, has been seen watching the men through the house door's iron grille. Bernarda calls her in and slaps her. She sends her daughters off to their rooms; and La Poncia tells Bernarda the men were talking about a village girl who was gang-raped the previous night.

We have a strong sense of a world where the double standard rules: men are allowed free expression of their sexuality, while women must repress theirs.

Bernarda goes to see the lawyer to discuss the terms of her late husband's will.

As an act of rebellion, Adela, the youngest, has changed into a green dress. The other sisters talk of the rumour that Pepe el

Romano, the most eligible bachelor of the district, is going to propose marriage to Angustias. Besides being the eldest, she is also the richest, because she inherits from her father, Bernarda's first husband. It becomes clear that Adela loves Pepe, and may be in a relationship with him, and that there is bitter rivalry between the sisters. The girls then rush off to catch a glimpse of Pepe walking down the street.

Bernarda sees Angustias with make-up on her face, and violently rubs it off. The sisters rush on to see what the conflict is. At that moment, María Josefa appears, dressed in faded finery. She's going to escape from this prison and live with a man by the shores of the sea. Bernarda and her daughters join to drag the mad, suffering old woman back into confinement.

Act Two   The sisters are doing their embroidery. All seems calm. Angustias's engagement to Pepe is now official. As custom dictates, he comes each night to converse with her through the metal grille of her window. Adela is in her room, alone; they all have noticed her agitation and distress. There is also an unexplained discrepancy around the time he leaves Angustias. She says it is around one a.m.; but others say he has been heard leaving at around four. The woman go off to see a travelling salesman who deals in lace.

Adela is left alone with La Poncia. She tells her she wants Pepe and means to have him. She will not allow anyone to stop her. La Poncia advises her to wait. Angustias is sickly and narrow-hipped. The first childbirth will kill her. Then Pepe will return for Adela. But Adela will not wait. It is clear she and Angustius are in a state of war.

The sisters return. It is midday. The heat suffocates. A gang of itinerant labourers have come to harvest the fields. They hired a prostitute the previous night. All hear them singing as they come back from the fields.

Angustias breaks the stillness in a state of fury. Someone has taken Pepe's photograph from her room. Bernarda orders La Poncia to search the girls' rooms. There is an expectation it will be found in Adela's; but it turns out it is the hunchbacked sister, Martirio, who has stolen it. Bernarda beats her, and there is an explosion of jealous fury betwen Martirio and Adela. Bernarda, in fury, sends the sisters back to their rooms.

Alone together, La Poncia hints to Bernarda about a scandal she suspects is about to break over Bernarda's head. Bernarda retaliates by reminding La Poncia of the knowledge she has of the scandal surrounding her – and fiercely asserts her confidence in her ability to control events. La Poncia artfully remarks that it's wonderful how keen Pepe is on his new fiancée, since he stays talking to her till four in the morning. Angustias denies this: Martirio corroborates it. We have a sense that the sisters have been overhearing everything; we know for sure that Adela has, in fact, been seeing Pepe; and we sense her secret is in danger of being revealed.

A tumult in the street diverts everyone's attention. Adela and Martirio snatch a moment together. Martirio also loves Pepe and is determined to prevent Adela having him. This is another declaration of open war.

The stage fills again as La La Poncia reveals what she has just heard: an unmarried girl in the village secretly gave birth to an illegitimate child and killed it to hide her shame. The village dogs uncovered the child's corpse from under a heap of stones. A mob is forming to lynch the mother. Adela clutches her belly. We know she is pregnant. Bernarda shouts at the mob to act fast before the police come – and urges them to kill the girl.

Act Three   All seems quiet again as the daughters eat their evening meal. Someone has come to visit; and from the woman's conventional words we catch a glimpse of a life lived in unresolved misery, whose anguish is tucked away out of sight – but never out of mind. The night is dark; the stars are big as fists; a stallion is trying to kick his way out of the stable.

Bernarda is sure she has the situation under control. But the talk between Bernarda and the maid after she has gone to bed suggests otherwise.

The Grandmother appears, singing to a baby lamb. Martirio persuades her back to bed in a scene of the profoundest fear and pathos. The hatred between Martirio and Adela is coming irresistibly out into the open, as is the fact that Adela and Pepe are having intercourse together. At a crucial moment of conflict between the two sisters, we hear a man whistle. It is Pepe; this is the signal for Adela to join him; Martirio prevents her leaving.

Martirio calls out for her mother. Bernarda appears. She moves
to strike Adela. But Adela grabs her mother's stick and breaks it.
Bernarda runs off for her rifle. We hear the gunshot. Martirio
comes back on stage to say Pepe has been shot dead. She is lying.
But Adela believes her and runs off, locking herself in her room.

Adela has hung herself. Bernarda orders her to be cut down. She
orders her daughters to stop weeping. She announces to the world
that her youngest daughter died a virgin. She imposes silence.
The play ends.

Sources

When Lorca was still a boy, he sometimes spent the summers with
his family in a small village called Asquerosa. Across the street
lived a domineering woman called Frasquita Alba Sierra, who
had married twice and had a total of seven children from her two
marriages. Lorca's cousins lived across the street from him, next
door to this woman's house. They shared a well with her at the
back of their houses; much of what went on in the Alba
household could be heard quite clearly and was passed onto the
Lorcas – and in particular to the fascinated young Federico.

It is very clear that this household, with its domineering mother,
its many daughters, their clashes with their mother over her
authority, and their disputes about who would eventually inherit
the family property, was the seed that, once planted in Federico's
imagination as a boy, was finally to grow into *The House of
Bernarda Alba* – this utterly extraordinary creation of the last
months of his life. Indeed, the resemblance between the Frasquita
Alba of the village and the Bernarda Alba of the play was so
close that it horrified Lorca's mother. She begged him to change
Bernarda's name so as not to offend the surviving members of
Frasquita's family. One theory even has it that the animosity
provoked by the resemblance between the names was so strong
that it was one of the factors that led to Lorca's assassination.

Because he never lived long enough to revise the play or have it
performed, we can only speculate as to whether he would have
agreed to his mother's request. What is for sure, though, is that
he took from his early memories of the village and its
surroundings much more than the name and basic

characteristics of this one household. The whole action of the play is rooted in the rural surroundings in which he grew up. In fact, in an early draft of the play, he described its setting as 'an Andalusian village on arid land'. This description precisely fits Asquerosa; and in many other respects the village of the play corresponds very closely to the village he knew as a child. 'Asquerosa' in Spanish means 'disgusting, loathsome', and in certain respects, at least, this seems to have been a place which lived up to its name. It was rife with gossip and with an utterly obsessive and often deeply damaging fascination with other people's lives; a place with a poisonous atmosphere, beautifully summed up by Bernarda herself where she talks of 'this wretched little village, without a river. This village of wells, where you're afraid to drink the water in case it's been poisoned.'

Many other details of life, as portrayed in the play, are authentic to the village: the incredibly long periods of mourning; the repressive sexual morality; the appalling, crushing heat; the arrival of the reapers in the summer from the hills. Even the language of the play is said to reflect the inhabitants' particular way of speaking. Many of the characters, too, are based on real people Lorca knew as a child. La Poncia was a real servant, although she never worked for Frasquita Alba. Bernarda's crazy old grandmother, María Josefa, was inspired by an aged relative Federico and his brother used to visit when they were children. The rejected suitor, Enrique Humanes, and the husband whose wife gets carried off to the olive grove were also people who existed in flesh and blood.

Adela's green dress was inspired by one of Lorca's favourite cousins, who also had a green dress she dearly loved and who, on one celebrated family occasion, could only show it off to the chickens in the backyard because the family was going through a period of mourning.

No doubt a more patient researcher could investigate many more incidents and characters in the play and discover many more links between them and Lorca's experience of life in the villages of Spain. And perhaps this is one of the reasons why Lorca prefaces the play with the words: 'The poet wishes to point out that these three acts are intended to be a photographic documentary.'

So before we even begin to experience the play we are invited to bear in mind that what it represents is actually true – on whatever level we may choose to interpret this. We may wonder why Lorca should choose such a subject: why so extraordinarily gifted and imaginative a poet should choose such an apparently unpoetic form.

It is certainly striking that Lorca should have chosen to return to these childhood roots after a life which, even the briefest summary indicates, took him far from his own roots in the Andalusian countryside. He left for Madrid when he was twenty-one, encountered the vibrant intellectual and artistic life of the capital, and had intense relationships with the film-maker Buñuel, the surrealist artist Salvador Dalí, and a dazzling group of young writers and poets. In 1928, the extraordinary success of his book of poems *The Gypsy Ballads* (*Romancero Gitano*) made him one of Spain's best-known poets. By 1929 he was in New York, where he witnessed the Wall Street Crash, and then made a triumphant lecture/recital tour of Cuba and South America. He was fascinated by surrealism, film-making, painting and jazz. Even this, the briefest of descriptions, should make it clear that this was a poet and artist open to influence from all over the globe. It is extraordinary that at the end of his life he should, in a sense, turn his back on all this and concentrate with an almost obsessive power and precision on scenes from his own childhood.

The House of Bernarda Alba, more than many of his other plays, is steeped in the personal, social and cultural contexts that helped shape it. To begin to understand it, we need to make an imaginative journey back into the author's past and, through that journey, make the connections that help us understand this play in the present.

Social Concerns

The wealthiest character in this play is perhaps also the one most thwarted in her life; and who, as a consequence, passionately devotes herself to thwarting the lives of others. Like the head of a Wall Street bank, Bernarda is portrayed as someone whose animal greed and savagery is only thinly masked by a veneer of conventional piety. She works constantly to increase her material wealth, as her neighbours' remarks reveal, and her avarice lies at the heart of the suffering she inflicts on herself and on others. It is a side of Bernarda that has been cannily perceived by the mad old María Josefa in her little rhyme: 'Bernarda's got a leopard's face'.

The comparative wealth possessed by the Alba family brings them no happiness. Instead, both mother and daughters seem trapped in a cage of their own making, in which they remain imprisoned by their own fear and their own sense of class values. This snobbery denies them any slight avenues of escape – such as marriage to Enrique Humanas for Martirio. Adela is the only one with the courage to attempt to break free: and that courage costs her her life.

The Play's Religious Dimension

When Lorca was a child, he was fascinated by the village church, and by its (still semi-pagan) festivals – one of which was the starting point for his earlier tragedy *Yerma*. Behind the church altar was a smiling image of the Virgin of Good Love (La Virgen del Buen Amor):

> When the organ started up my soul was in ecstasy and I fixed my eyes tenderly on the child Jesus and the Virgin of Good Love, always loving and a little silly with her tin crown, stars and spangles. When the organ started up, the smoke of the incense and the tinkling of the little bells excited me, and I would become terrified of sins which no longer concern me.

His fascination with religion spilled over into the games Lorca used to play at home. A childhood friend remembered how he created a little shrine to the Virgin in the backyard of his house, decorated it with flowers from the garden, dressed up in a variety of finery from the dressing-up box in the attic and pretended to say mass to family and friends with the most profound conviction. The climax of the service was his sermon: and he insisted that everyone cried.

Lorca retained a profound concern with religion throughout his life, though as he grew older he came to detest many aspects of the Catholic Church; a rage that was to attain magnificent expression in the poem 'Cry to Rome'. This is an amazing denunciation not only of the savage cruelty and inhumanity of the capitalist system Lorca saw operating in New York, but of the complacency of a Catholic Church that refuses to disengage itself from such corruption and which has, in consequence, utterly lost touch with its spirituality.

A similar rage informs the church imagery used in *The House of Bernarda Alba*. The play begins with a church service, whose bells are heard offstage. But the tinkling of little bells that aroused the soul of the young Lorca to ecstasy have here been transformed into a heavy symbol of physical and emotional repression:

> Bloody bells! Going round and round my head!

The very first line spoken in the play, then, sets the scene for a kind of distorted Passion Play whose central figure, Bernarda, a kind of Virgin of Bad Love, destroys the sexuality and the lives of herself and all around her. She presides over a house which La Poncia significantly refers to as a 'convent' – a convent dedicated not to the love of God or concern for mankind but to cruelty and repression masquerading as a kind of sacrilegious piety.

By this late stage in his career, Lorca's loathing for reactionary elements in the Catholic Church had become reciprocal; following the opening of his play *Yerma* in 1934, Lorca had come to be viewed as an enemy of the church. There's no question that his targets in *Bernarda Alba* were those same repressive Church authorities enjoying and abusing a centuries-old position of privilege.

He presents us, in *The House of Bernarda Alba*, with a world dominated by piety at its most oppressive; Christ, however, is not altogether absent from this world. Adela expresses her final act of rebellion in terms which powerfully remind us of his passion:

> Even if all the so-called respectable people in this so-called respectable village pursue me and hunt me down, I'll still stand by him. Openly and without shame. And I'll gladly wear my crown of thorns.

This deliberate association of sexual freedom with the figure of Jesus Christ is something that must continue to shock the conservatively minded. In his own imagination, perhaps, Lorca is still dressed as a priest, preaching a sermon: a sermon of human liberation.

The House of Bernarda Alba on Stage

The first public performance of *The House of Bernarda Alba* took place on 8 March 1945 in the Teatro Avenida in Buenos Aires, where it was performed by Margarita Xirgu and her company. It was, however, another nineteen years before it became possible to get it past the censors of Franco's Spain and was performed in Madrid on 10 January 1964 at the Teatre Goya.

Since then it has gone on to become one of the most-often performed of Lorca's plays, and its theatrical history has been skilfully summarised in Maria Delgado's excellent study of Lorca as a dramatist.

Notable productons in Spain include Calixto Bieito's abstract staging for Madrid's Centro Dramático Nacional in 1998. He set the play in an austere, empty space, dominated by chairs, and overhung by a nude aerialist whose contortions counterpointed the protagonists' sexual frustrations.

In many respects the play's dramatic world is intensely alien to the world of British theatre, and this presents many difficulties to stagings of the play in English. It's very easy, for instance, for English-language productions to get themselves tangled up in the British class system. Hard to convey Bernarda's upper-class pretensions without sounding terribly Home Counties; difficult to convey the searing heat of the house's interior in chilly British springs and summers; perhaps impossible to convey to an urban British audience the restrictions placed on rural Spanish women's lives.

None of this has prevented many different productions on the British stage. Perhaps the most celebrated English-language production took place in the Lyric Theatre Hammersmith in the early 1980s. Translated by Robert David MacDonald and directed by Nuria Espert, it starred Joan Plowright and Glenda Jackson in the leading roles, was immensely successful and transferred to the West End.

Polly Teale's staging of Rona Munro's version for Shared Experience in 1999 took the play on a wide-ranging English tour that opened in Salisbury and played throughout the country before ending up in London's Young Vic.

In spite of the difficulties, which English-language productions have arguably never fully resolved, the play has a visceral resonance and power that mean it continually cries out to be staged.

To Conclude

Lorca's remarkable theatre-writing skills are astonishingly present in every word of *The House of Bernarda Alba*. Lorca wrote of it, 'I've had to cut a lot of things in this tragedy. I cut out a lot of facile songs and little rhymes. I want the work to have a severe simplicity.' The dialogue is of an incredible economy and power; its emotional intensity is such that just reading it in the Spanish is enough to send shivers up the spine. Perhaps even more remarkable is the immaculate structure that underpins the dialogue; the way he has imperceptibly telescoped events that would normally have taken a few weeks, without losing that sense of urgency and speed that great tragedy demands.

He wrote it for the very great actress, Margarita Xirgu, with whom he had collaborated over many years and for whom he wrote so much of his work: *Mariana Pineda*, *Doña Rosita the Spinster*, *Blood Wedding*, *Yerma*. If you write for the theatre, inevitably you are influenced by who you are writing for; there is no question about the fact that Xirgu must have influenced Lorca and been at least partly responsible for the amazing range of excellent female parts he wrote for the stage.

Lorca was also a homosexual, who had the misfortune to live in a country where, and at a time when, male homosexuality was considered deeply shameful. He was denied the right to express his sexuality openly in his life; denied, too, the right to explore it or express it openly in his work. It seems very obvious that the grotesquely unjust and unnecessary suffering he had to endure as a result deepened his own identification with women denied control over their own bodies and access to their own sexuality.

In *Bernarda Alba* this oppression is seen at its most extreme. Lorca warned that the play should not just be taken as a metaphor; another reason why he wrote on the title page that the play should be considered a 'photographic documentary'.

At first sight, he seems to be presenting us with a very remote and alien world, but the worst mistake we could make, either in watching or presenting it, would be to treat it as a kind of curiosity, the theatrical equivalent of a tourist trip to an exotic location. For all of us have our Bernarda somewhere inside us: our own monstrous tyrant of conformity and shame that inhibits so much of our human and creative impulse.

Lorca finished the play in the summer of 1936; he read it aloud to friends, as was his custom, and then left Madrid for his habitual summer vacation in his home town of Granada. He took the manuscript with him, along with the toy theatre that he took everywhere on his travels. He was mildly worried about how the play would be received, and how people would take the fact that it had no men in it. He had written one of the truly great works of this century; it is oddly endearing to find him worried about it.

He intended to revise it, but never had the time. Civil war broke out, the fascist authorities took him away and had him shot. He was thirty-eight years old. For, as Lorca was writing the play, an army general called Francisco Franco, with his head stuffed with dead ideas, was preparing a revolution. Lorca may not have consciously known it, but he was writing under the shadow of death.

All of us now watching *Bernarda Alba* watch under a shadow of our own. Authorities parrot nonsense at us, dazzle us with intellectually void and morally bankrupt talk of 'profitability' and 'enterprise'. Old and moribund ideas, ideas which should have died with the nineteenth century, still haunt us and threaten our environment and our lives, even if they are dressed up with words like 'modernisation'. We may imagine the threat to be remote. So did Lorca. Threats have a habit of seeming unreal until it is too late to avert them. We have to take the play as a warning: we have to learn.

Note

The present translation was first presented at the Royal Lyceum Theatre in Edinburgh in May 1989 and has been revised for publication here.

The play was subsequently produced by Graeae Theatre Company and the Royal Exchange Theatre, and first performed at the Royal Exchange Theatre, Manchester, on 3 February 2017.

The production was directed by Jenny Sealey and starred Kathryn Hunter as Bernarda Alba.

For Further Reading

The experience of translating Lorca always leaves me profoundly aware of the deficiencies of any translation. Those wishing to make contact with the plays in their original language should use these editions as their starting point: *Bodas de sangre*, edited by H. Ramsden, Manchester University Press, 1980; *Yerma*, edited by Robin Warner, Manchester University Press, 1994, and *La casa de Bernarda Alba*, edited by H. Ramsden, Manchester University Press, 1984.

The best guide to Lorca's life is Ian Gibson's magnificent biography: *Federico García Lorca: A Life*, Faber, 1989.

A good academic introduction to Lorca's plays is Gwynne Edwards' *The Theatre Beneath the Sand*, Marion Boyars, 1989.

Gay themes in Lorca's work are explored in *Lorca and the Gay Imagination* by Paul Binding, GMP Books, 1985.

There are a great many available translations of Lorca's poetry. One of the best is *Poet in New York* (bilingual edition), translated by Greg Simon and Steven F. White, Viking, 1988.

An interesting collection of essays and creative responses, including discussions of the problems of translating Lorca is *Fire, Blood and the Alphabet: One Hundred Years of Lorca*, ed. Doggart and Thompson, Durham University Press, 2000.

BLOOD WEDDING

Characters

THE MOTHER
THE BRIDE-TO-BE (*later* THE BRIDE)
THE MOTHER-IN-LAW
LEONARDO'S WIFE
THE MAID
THE NEIGHBOUR
GIRLS
LEONARDO
THE BRIDEGROOM
THE FATHER OF THE BRIDE-TO-BE
THE MOON
YOUNG MEN
WOODCUTTERS
THE MOON
THE BEGGARWOMAN (DEATH)

ACT ONE

Scene One

A room painted yellow.

BRIDEGROOM (*coming in*). Mother.

MOTHER. What?

BRIDEGROOM. I'm going.

MOTHER. Where?

BRIDEGROOM. To the vineyard. (*About to leave.*)

MOTHER. Wait.

BRIDEGROOM. What do you want?

MOTHER. I want to give you some food to take.

BRIDEGROOM. Don't bother. I'll eat grapes. Give me the knife.

MOTHER. Why?

BRIDEGROOM (*laughing*). To cut them off the vine.

MOTHER (*muttering as she looks for it*). Knives . . . knives . . . I curse them. Curse them all and the criminals who make them.

BRIDEGROOM. Let's talk of something else.

MOTHER. And machine guns and pistols and knives and sickles and scythes.

BRIDEGROOM. That's enough.

MOTHER. Everything with a blade that can cut open the body of a man. A beautiful man, with a mouth like a flower. A man who goes out to his vines or his fields or his olive groves because they are his . . .

BRIDEGROOM (*lowering his head*). Be quiet. Please . . .

MOTHER. . . . . and then never returns. Or if he does, if he does come back it's only so we can cover his head with a shroud or cover him with salt to stop his corpse swelling. I don't know how you dare carry a knife in your belt or why I keep one in my house. It's like keeping a snake.

BRIDEGROOM. Haven't you said enough?

MOTHER. No. I'll never say enough. Not even if I lived to be a hundred. First they killed your father who smelt like a rose. I only enjoyed him three years. Then they killed your brother. And is it right and is it just that something as small as a pistol or a knife can finish off a man? A man is a bull, it should take more than such a tiny thing. So no. I'll never be silent. Months pass. Years pass, and despair bites into me. I can feel it gnawing. At the back of my eyes. At the roots of my hair.

BRIDEGROOM (*fiercely*). Will this never end?

MOTHER. No. No, this will never end. Can anyone bring your father back? Anyone bring back your brother? And people talk of jail. But what's that? They can eat there. The murderers. They can eat there, and smoke if they want, and play their guitars. And my two dead bodies turning into grass. Slowly turning into grass. With no voice in their heads. Only dust. Two men once fresh as flowers. While the murderers live in jail. Cool as cucumbers. With a view of the mountains . . .

BRIDEGROOM. So you want me to kill them?

MOTHER. No. No, I'm only talking because . . . They went out that door. How can I bear to see you go out of it too? And I don't like you carrying a knife. It's just . . . I hate you going out the house.

BRIDEGROOM. The nonsense you talk.

MOTHER. I wish you were a girl. Then you'd stay at home and we'd do the sewing together. We'd embroider tablecloths and knit woolly jumpers for the winter.

BRIDEGROOM (*taking the* MOTHER *by the arm, and laughing*). Mother, what if I took you with me to the vineyard?

MOTHER. And what would an old woman do in the vineyard? Would you lie with me under the grapes?

BRIDEGROOM (*picking her up in his arms*). You? You old old old old old woman, you.

MOTHER. Your father used to take me. Yes. There was a man for you. Good stock. Your grandfather left a child in every street corner. That's how it should be. Men being men. Grass being grass.

BRIDEGROOM. Mother. What about me?

MOTHER. What about you?

BRIDEGROOM. Have I got to explain it all over again?

MOTHER (*gravely*). That.

BRIDEGROOM. Do you think it's a bad idea?

MOTHER. No.

BRIDEGROOM. Well then?

MOTHER. I'm not sure I really know. You bring it up like that, all of a sudden, and it throws me. I know the girl is good. And that's right, isn't it? I know she's got good manners, and I know she's a good worker. She can bake her own bread and sew her own clothes and yet whenever I think of her name it's as if my head was being hit by a stone.

BRIDEGROOM. That's ridiculous.

MOTHER. No. It's not ridiculous. It's just I'll be left on my own. You're all that I've got left and I don't want you to go.

BRIDEGROOM. But you'll come with us.

MOTHER. No. I can't leave your father and your brother here on their own. I have to go and see them every morning. Because if I didn't, one of that family of murderers, one of the Felix, one of them could die and they might bury them beside my dead. And I couldn't bear that. Never. Never! Because I would have to dig them up with my fingernails and smash their bones against a wall.

BRIDEGROOM (*angrily*). And now you've started. Again.

MOTHER. I'm sorry. (*Pause.*) How long have you been seeing her?

BRIDEGROOM. Three years. Enough time to buy the vineyard.

MOTHER. Three years. Wasn't she once going to marry someone else?

BRIDEGROOM. I don't know. I don't think so. Girls have to think hard about who they're going to marry.

MOTHER. No. No, they don't. I never thought. I never looked at anyone. I looked at your father. And then when they killed him I looked at the neighbour's wall. A woman can have just the one man. And that's all.

BRIDEGROOM. You know that she's a good girl.

MOTHER. I'm sure she is. I just wish I knew who her mother was.

BRIDEGROOM. What difference does that make?

MOTHER (*looking at him*). My son.

BRIDEGROOM. Now what do you want?

MOTHER. To tell you you're right. That I believe you! When do you want me to call on them?

BRIDEGROOM (*happily*). What about Sunday?

MOTHER (*seriously*). I'll take her the brass earrings, because they're antiques, and you'll buy her . . .

BRIDEGROOM. You'll know what's best . . .

MOTHER. You buy her some fancy stockings, and two new suits for you . . . Not two. Three! You're all I have!

BRIDEGROOM. I'm off. I'll go see her tomorrow.

MOTHER. Yes, of course, you go, and you see if you can't give me six grandchildren to make me happy. Boys or girls, whatever you want, but grandchildren. Because your father never had the time to give me some.

BRIDEGROOM. The first one is yours.

MOTHER. Yes. But make sure you have girls. Because I want to embroider and sew and live in peace.

BRIDEGROOM. I am sure you'll love my new wife.

MOTHER. Of course I will. (*Goes to kiss him and then changes her mind.*) No. You're too grown-up for kisses. Save them for your wife. (*Pause. Aside.*) Assuming she ever marries you.

BRIDEGROOM. I'm away.

MOTHER. Work on that patch by the mill. You've been neglecting it.

BRIDEGROOM. Whatever you say.

MOTHER. Go with God.

The BRIDEGROOM *goes. The* MOTHER *stays where she is: sitting with her back to the door. A* NEIGHBOUR *appears in the doorway dressed in a dark colour, with a handkerchief covering her head.*

Come in.

NEIGHBOUR. How are you?

MOTHER. As you see.

NEIGHBOUR. I came down to the shop and thought I'd come in to see you. We live so far away!

MOTHER. It's twenty years since I went to the top of the street.

NEIGHBOUR. You're lucky.

MOTHER. You think so?

NEIGHBOUR. The things that happen. Just the other day they brought in my neighbour's son with both his arms cut off. (*She sits.*)

MOTHER. Rafael?

NEIGHBOUR. Yes. Rafael. It was the machine. And there he is. I often think that our two dead sons are better off where they are, asleep and at rest, rather than risking ending up maimed and useless.

MOTHER. Be quiet. That's just something people say. It doesn't help.

NEIGHBOUR. No.

MOTHER. No. (*Pause.*)

NEIGHBOUR (*sadly*). How's your son?

MOTHER. He went out.

NEIGHBOUR. He finally managed to buy the vineyard!

MOTHER. He was lucky.

NEIGHBOUR. He can get married now.

MOTHER (*as if waking up, and bringing her chair closer to the NEIGHBOUR's*). Listen.

NEIGHBOUR (*ready to receive a confidence*). Tell me.

MOTHER. Do you know the girl my son wants to marry?

NEIGHBOUR. She's a good girl!

MOTHER. Yes, but . . .

NEIGHBOUR. It's true there's no one really knows her well. She lives out there alone with her father, in the middle of nowhere, ten miles from the nearest house. But she's a good girl. Used to being alone.

MOTHER. What about her mother?

NEIGHBOUR. She was beautiful. Her face shone. I knew her. But I never liked her. She didn't love her husband.

MOTHER (*fiercely*). The things you know about people!

NEIGHBOUR. I'm sorry. I didn't mean to cause offence. It's true though. Now, as to whether she behaved as she should, or not, there's no telling. She was always proud. And no one ever said anything.

MOTHER. Like mother, like daughter.

NEIGHBOUR. You were the one who asked.

MOTHER. It's just that I'd like no one to know them. Not to know the living daughter, not to know the dead mother. I'd like them to be blank walls people pass without seeing.

NEIGHBOUR. You're right. Your son is worth so much.

MOTHER. That's why I take such care of him. Someone told me that a while ago the girl was going to marry someone else.

NEIGHBOUR. That would have been when she was fifteen. He got married two years ago. Married one of her cousins. I'm sure of it. He used to go out with her. But now no one remembers that.

MOTHER. Then how come you remember it?

NEIGHBOUR. Because you asked me!

MOTHER. We all need to find out things that hurt us. Who was the boy?

NEIGHBOUR. Leonardo.

MOTHER. What Leonardo?

NEIGHBOUR. Leonardo Felix.

MOTHER (*getting up*). Felix!

NEIGHBOUR. Listen, he's got nothing to do with anything. It wasn't his fault. He was just a boy when the troubles came. A boy of eight.

MOTHER. You're right . . . Of course you are. It's just when I hear that name, Felix, it's as if when I say it, (*Under her breath.*) Felix, it's as if my mouth is filling with my husband's ashes (*Spits.*) and I have to spit, I have to keep spitting or I'll kill someone.

NEIGHBOUR. Calm down. You can't go on thinking like this. No good will come of it.

MOTHER. No. But you know what I'm saying.

NEIGHBOUR. Don't get in the way of your son's happiness. Don't tell him. You're an old woman. And I am too. It's best we keep our mouths shut.

MOTHER. I won't tell him anything.

NEIGHBOUR (*kissing her*). Say nothing.

MOTHER (*calmly*). Life!

NEIGHBOUR. I'm away. My people will be coming back from the field.

MOTHER. Have you seen how hot it is?

NEIGHBOUR. The boys taking water to the harvesters were roasting. Goodbye.

MOTHER. Go with God.

The MOTHER *heads for the door on the left. Halfway across she stops and slowly crosses herself.*

Curtain.

Scene Two

A room painted pink with copper pans and vases of flowers. In the centre, a table with a tablecloth. It is morning.

LEONARDO's MOTHER-IN-LAW *with a baby in her arms. She rocks it. The* WIFE, *in the other corner, does her embroidery.*

MOTHER-IN-LAW. Hush, little baby
  For the horse at the stream
  Black is the water
  That flows like a dream
  The horse she is thirsty
  The water black as ink
  The horse she is thirsty
  But refuses to drink
  What's wrong with the water
  What's wrong with the horse?

WIFE (*speaking low*). Sleep, little flower
  For the horse that won't drink

MOTHER-IN-LAW. Sleep, little rosebud
  For the horse starts to weep
  Its hooves they are wounded
  Its mane is of ice
  A dagger of silver
  Has pierced its great eye.
  They go down to the river,
  Oh, how they go down!
  The water flows deeply
  But in blood they can drown.

WIFE. Sleep, little flower
  For the horse that won't drink

MOTHER-IN-LAW. Sleep, little rose
  For the horse starts to weep.

WIFE. Its muzzle is burning
  And buzzing with flies
  If it touches the river
  The horse surely dies
  It cries out to the mountains

It cries out to the marsh
Cries out to the river
In a voice loud and harsh
Cry for the horsey
That can't bear to drink
Cry for the river
With water black as ink.

MOTHER-IN-LAW. Don't come through the window
Don't come through the door!
We'll lock up the window
With trees and with dreams
And we'll bolt up the door
The horse by the river
Won't come any more.

WIFE. My boy, he is sleeping

MOTHER-IN-LAW. My boy, he is still

WIFE. My boy, has a pillow
With down soft as silk.

MOTHER-IN-LAW. He has a steel cradle

WIFE. Sheets white as milk

MOTHER-IN-LAW. Hush, little baby

WIFE. For the horse that won't drink!

MOTHER-IN-LAW. Don't come through the window
Don't come through the door!
Go up to the mountain
Where the valley is grey
The horse by the fountain
That thirsts all the day.

WIFE (*looking*). My baby is sleeping

MOTHER-IN-LAW. My baby's asleep

WIFE (*very low*). Sleep, little flower
For the horse that won't drink

MOTHER-IN-LAW (*getting up and speaking very low*).
Sleep, little rose
For the horse starts to weep.

They take the child off. LEONARDO *comes on.*

LEONARDO. How's the baby?

WIFE. Fast asleep.

LEONARDO. Yesterday he wasn't well. He cried all night.

WIFE (*happily*). Today he's like a flower. How about you?
  Did you go to the blacksmith's?

LEONARDO. I've just come from there. Could you believe it?
  I've spent the last two months putting new shoes on that horse
  and they still keep falling off. Apparently they get torn off by
  the stones.

WIFE. Won't it be because you ride so far?

LEONARDO. No. I hardly ever ride it.

WIFE. The neighbours told me yesterday that they saw you at the
  far end of the salt flats.

LEONARDO. Who said that?

WIFE. The women picking capers. I couldn't believe it. Was it
  really you?

LEONARDO. No. What would I be doing there, out in that
  desert?

WIFE. That's what I said. But then the horse was half-dead with
  weariness.

LEONARDO. Did you see it?

WIFE. No. But my mother did.

LEONARDO. Is she with the baby?

WIFE. Yes. Do you want a drink?

LEONARDO. Make it really cold.

WIFE. You never came in to eat! . . .

LEONARDO. I was with the men who were weighing the wheat.
  They're always good for a laugh.

WIFE (*very gently, as she makes the drink*). And do they pay a good
  price?

LEONARDO. Just what's right.

WIFE. I need a new dress and the baby a new sun hat.

LEONARDO (*getting up*). I'll go in to see him.

WIFE. Careful. He's fast asleep.

MOTHER-IN-LAW (*coming in*). Someone's been riding that horse into the ground. It's lying half-dead in the stable with its eyes starting out of its head. Who would have done such a thing?

LEONARDO (*bitterly*). I did.

MOTHER-IN-LAW. I do beg your pardon. After all, it is your horse.

WIFE (*timidly*). He was with the men measuring the wheat.

MOTHER-IN-LAW. I don't care where he said he was. (*She sits down. Pause.*)

WIFE. Your drink. Was it cold enough?

LEONARDO. Yes.

WIFE. Have you heard my cousin's going to get married?

LEONARDO. When?

WIFE. They're coming to arrange it tomorrow. The wedding's going to be next month. I hope they invite us.

LEONARDO (*seriously*). I'm not so sure.

MOTHER-IN-LAW. I've heard that the boy's mother isn't very happy with the marriage.

LEONARDO. I don't blame her. You can't trust the girl.

WIFE. I hate you thinking badly of a good girl.

MOTHER-IN-LAW (*maliciously*). He just says that because he knows her. Don't you know he went out with her for three years?

LEONARDO. But I left her. (*To his* WIFE.) Now you're going to cry. Stop! (*He brusquely takes her hands away from her face.*) Let's go and see the baby.

They go in arm in arm. The GIRL *arrives, happily. She runs in.*

GIRL. You should see what's going on!

MOTHER-IN-LAW. And what's that?

GIRL. The new husband's come to the shop and he's bought the best of everything.

MOTHER-IN-LAW. Did he come on his own?

GIRL. No, he came with his mother. She's very tall. Very serious. (*She imitates her*). And very extravagant! The things they bought!

MOTHER-IN-LAW. They're rich.

GIRL. And they bought the most gorgeous stockings! . . . They were so lovely! The kind of stocking you dream of! The embroidery was so beautiful. Imagine: a swallow here (*pointing to her ankle*). A sailing ship here (*pointing to her calf*), and here there was a beautiful rose (*pointing to her thigh*).

MOTHER-IN-LAW. Don't be rude!

GIRL. But you should have seen it! A rose with its petals and its thorn! All in silk!

MOTHER-IN-LAW. They're uniting two very good going concerns.

LEONARDO *and his* WIFE *appear.*

GIRL. I came to tell you what they bought.

LEONARDO (*fiercely*). We don't want to know.

WIFE. Let her tell us.

MOTHER-IN-LAW. Leonardo, there's no need for that.

GIRL. I'm sorry. (*She goes, crying.*)

MOTHER-IN-LAW. Why do you always have to be mean to people?

LEONARDO. I never asked for your opinion. (*He sits.*)

MOTHER-IN-LAW. Very well. (*Pause.*)

WIFE (*to* LEONARDO). What's wrong with you? What's going on in your mind? You just can't leave it like this, without telling me anything . . .

LEONARDO. Stop it.

WIFE. No. I want you to look me in the eyes and tell me.

LEONARDO. Leave me alone. (*He gets up.*)

WIFE. Where are you going?

LEONARDO (*bitterly*). Be quiet!

MOTHER-IN-LAW (*fiercely, to her daughter*). Be quiet!
(LEONARDO *goes*). The baby!

She exits and re-enters with the baby in her arms. The WIFE *has stayed
standing, absolutely still.*

Its hooves they are wounded
Its mane is of ice
A sharp silver dagger
Has pierced its soft eyes.
They go down to the river,
Oh, how they went down!
The water flows deeply
In the blood they will drown.

WIFE (*slowly coming back to herself and as if in a dream*).
Sleep, little flower
The horse starts to drink

MOTHER-IN-LAW. Sleep, little rosebud
The horse starts to weep.

WIFE. Sleep, baby, sleep.

MOTHER-IN-LAW. The poor big horse
That didn't want to drink!

WIFE (*full of feeling*). Don't enter the window
Don't come in by the door!
Go back to the mountain!
The snow bleeds on the mountain
In the pain of the dawn!

MOTHER-IN-LAW (*crying*). My baby is sleeping . . .

WIFE (*crying and slowly approaching*). My baby's at rest . . .

MOTHER-IN-LAW. Sleep, little flower
For the horse that won't drink

WIFE (*crying and leaning against the table*). Sleep, little rose
For the horse starts to weep.

Scene Three

Interior of the cave where the BRIDE-TO-BE *lives. In the rear, a rosy cross made of big flowers. The doors are round with lace curtains and pink ribbons. Harsh white material covers the walls, round fans, blue jars, and small mirrors.*

MAID. Come in . . . (*Very friendly, full of false humility.*)

The BRIDEGROOM *and his* MOTHER *come in. The* MOTHER *is dressed in black satin and wears a lace mantilla. The* BRIDEGROOM *in black corduroy with a big gold watch chain.*

Do you want to sit down? They're just coming.

She goes out. MOTHER *and the* BRIDEGROOM *sit as still as statues. Long pause.*

MOTHER. Have you got your watch?

BRIDEGROOM. Yes. (*He takes it out and looks at it.*)

MOTHER. We've got to get back in time. These people live so far away!

BRIDEGROOM. But this is good land.

MOTHER. Yes, good land. But too far away. Four hours' journey without a house or a tree.

BRIDEGROOM. These are the dry lands.

MOTHER. Your father would have covered them with trees.

BRIDEGROOM. Without water?

MOTHER. He'd have found some. The three years we were married he planted ten cherry trees. (*Remembering.*) The three walnut trees by the mill, a whole new vine, and a plant that's called Jupiter and gives scarlet flowers and dried out and died. (*Pause.*)

BRIDEGROOM (*of the* BRIDE-TO-BE). She must be getting dressed.

The FATHER *comes in. He is an old man, with shining white hair. His head is lowered. The* MOTHER *and the* BRIDEGROOM *get up, and they shake hands in silence.*

FATHER. Did you have a long journey?

MOTHER. Four hours.

They sit.

FATHER. You must have come the long way round.

MOTHER. I'm too old to go traipsing over the rough country by the river.

BRIDEGROOM. She gets travel-sick. (*Pause.*)

FATHER. It's been a good year for esparto.

BRIDEGROOM. Really excellent.

FATHER. In my day, this country wouldn't even yield esparto. It's had to be punished. It's even had to be cried over to get any good out of it.

MOTHER. But now you're getting the good. So don't complain. I haven't come to ask anything of you.

FATHER (*smiling*). You're richer than I am. Your vines are worth a fortune. Every bunch of grapes is like a heap of silver. The only thing that bothers me is that our land is split up. Do you understand? I like everything joined up. One thing that really hurts me, and it's like a thorn in my heart, is this little market garden in the middle of my land that the owner refuses to sell. And he won't let me buy it for all the gold in the world.

BRIDEGROOM. That sort of thing always happens.

FATHER. If only we could hook up twenty pairs of oxen and drag your land over here next to mine. How wonderful that would be.

MOTHER. Why?

FATHER. Because what's mine is hers and what's yours is his. Because of that. And to have it all together. To have it all together would be so beautiful.

BRIDEGROOM. And less work.

MOTHER. When I'm dead, you can sell all the land over there and buy more here.

FATHER. Sell? Sell! No, don't sell. Buy. Buy everything. If I'd had sons I'd have bought all this mountain right over to the stream. Because it's not good land. But with hard work you can make it good, and since people don't come here no one's going to rob your orchards and you can sleep in peace. (*Pause.*)

MOTHER. You know why I have come.

FATHER. Yes.

MOTHER. And what do you think?

FATHER. It seems good to me. They've spoken about it.

MOTHER. My son has and can.

FATHER. My daughter too.

MOTHER. My son is handsome. He has known no other woman. His reputation is as spotless as a sheet put out to dry in the sun.

FATHER. What can I tell you about my daughter? She gets up at three to make the men's breakfast. She never speaks. She's as soft as wool, she can do every kind of embroidery and she can cut a rope with her teeth.

MOTHER. May God bless her house.

FATHER. May God bless it.

The MAID *appears with two trays. One with glasses; one with sweets.*

MOTHER (*to her son*). When do you want to hold the wedding?

BRIDEGROOM. Next Thursday.

FATHER. That's her birthday. She'll be twenty-two years old.

MOTHER. Twenty-two years old! That's how old my eldest son would be if he were still alive. And he'd be warm and virile, if only men hadn't invented knives.

FATHER. You shouldn't think about it.

MOTHER. But I do. Every minute of every day. You would do the same.

FATHER. Thursday then. Right?

BRIDEGROOM. Right.

FATHER. The four of us will go in a car to church, which is a long way away, and all the guests can come in their carts and on the horses they bring.

MOTHER. Agreed.

The MAID *passes through.*

FATHER. Tell her she can come in now. (*To the* MOTHER.) I so hope you like her.

The BRIDE-TO-BE *appears. Her hands are folded modestly together and she keeps her gaze lowered.*

MOTHER. Come here. Are you happy?

BRIDE-TO-BE. Very happy.

FATHER. You don't look happy. Don't be so serious. At the end of the day she's going to be your mother.

BRIDE-TO-BE. I am happy. When I said yes it was because I wanted to.

MOTHER. Of course. (*She holds her by the chin*). Look at me.

FATHER. She's the spitting image of her mother.

MOTHER. Is she? What beautiful eyes! You dear creature, do you know what marriage is?

BRIDE-TO-BE (*gravely*). I know.

MOTHER. A man, some sons, and a wall. A wall six-feet deep to shut out the world.

BRIDEGROOM. What else could anyone want?

MOTHER. Nothing. Let them all live. That above all. Let them live!

BRIDE-TO-BE. I'll do what's expected.

MOTHER. Here are some presents.

BRIDE-TO-BE. Thank you.

FATHER. Won't we drink something?

MOTHER. I want nothing. (*To the* BRIDEGROOM.) What about you?

BRIDEGROOM. I'll have one of these. (*He takes a sweet. The* BRIDE-TO-BE *takes another.*)

FATHER (*to the* BRIDEGROOM). Some wine?

MOTHER. He never drinks.

FATHER. All the better. (*Pause. Everyone is standing.*)

BRIDEGROOM (*to the* BRIDE-TO-BE). I'll come tomorrow.

BRIDE-TO-BE. At what time?

FATHER. At five.

BRIDE-TO-BE. I'll be waiting.

BRIDEGROOM. When I leave your side I feel as if I'm empty and have got a knot in my throat.

BRIDE-TO-BE. When you're my husband you won't have that.

BRIDEGROOM. That's what I tell myself.

MOTHER. Let's go. The sun won't wait. (*To the* FATHER.) Do we agree?

FATHER. We agree.

MOTHER (*to the* MAID). Goodbye.

MAID. Go with God.

The MOTHER *kisses the* BRIDE-TO-BE *and they leave silently.*

MOTHER (*at the door*). Goodbye, daughter.

The BRIDE-TO-BE *replies with a gesture.*

FATHER. I'll come out with you.

They exit.

MAID. I'm dying to see the presents.

BRIDE-TO-BE (*bitterly*). Don't touch.

MAID. Oh, come on, show me.

BRIDE-TO-BE. Don't want to.

MAID. At least show me the stockings. They say they're embroidered. Come on!

BRIDE-TO-BE. No.

MAID. For goodness' sake. It's not that bad. It's as if you didn't want to get married.

BRIDE-TO-BE (*biting her hand in her rage*). No.

MAID. Sweetheart, what's happening? Are you going to miss living like a queen? Don't think of bitterness. What reason have you got? None. Come on, let's see the presents. (*She grabs the box.*)

BRIDE-TO-BE (*grabbing her by the wrists*). Let go.

MAID. For heaven's sake!

BRIDE-TO-BE. I said let go.

MAID. You're stronger than a man.

BRIDE-TO-BE. Haven't I worked as a man? I wish I was one!

MAID. Don't say such things.

BRIDE-TO-BE. Quiet. I've said it. Let's talk about something else.

Light slowly drains from the stage. A long pause.

MAID. Did you hear a horse last night?

BRIDE-TO-BE. When?

MAID. About three.

BRIDE-TO-BE. It must have been a horse that broke away from the herd.

MAID. No. It had a rider.

BRIDE-TO-BE. How do you know?

MAID. Because I saw him. He stopped under your window. I was really shocked.

BRIDE-TO-BE. It was the man I'm going to marry. Sometimes he goes past at that time.

MAID. It wasn't him.

BRIDE-TO-BE. Did you see him?

MAID. Yes.

BRIDE-TO-BE. Then who was it?

MAID. It was Leonardo.

BRIDE-TO-BE (*fiercely*). Liar. Liar! Why should he come here?

MAID. He came.

BRIDE-TO-BE. Be quiet. A curse on your tongue.

The sound of a horse can be heard.

MAID (*at the window*). Look. Look! Was it him?

BRIDE-TO-BE. It was. It was him!

Rapid curtain.

ACT TWO

Scene One

Vestibule in the BRIDE-TO-BE*'s house. To the rear, a doorway. It is night. The* BRIDE-TO-BE *enters, wearing white tiered petticoats full of lacework and embroidery, and a white bodice which leaves her arms bare. The* MAID *is with her, wearing the same.*

MAID. I'll finish combing you here.

BRIDE-TO-BE. It's so hot inside. It's unbearable.

MAID. In these parts it never even gets cool at dawn.

The BRIDE-TO-BE *sits down in a low seat and looks at herself in a little hand mirror. The* MAID *combs her hair.*

BRIDE-TO-BE. My mother came from a place where there were so many trees. Fertile country. Full of water.

MAID. She overflowed with happiness.

BRIDE-TO-BE. But it burnt up here.

MAID. That's just how it is.

BRIDE-TO-BE. Just as we'll all burn up. It's like an oven in here. Fire comes out the walls. Ow. Don't pull so hard.

MAID. I want to get this wave just right. I want it to fall over your forehead. (*The* BRIDE-TO-BE *looks at herself in the mirror.*) You are so beautiful! (*She kisses her passionately.*)

BRIDE-TO-BE (*seriously*). Don't stop combing me.

MAID (*combing her*). You're so lucky. You're going to kiss a man. You're going to embrace him. You're going to feel his weight on you.

BRIDE-TO-BE. Shut up.

MAID. And the best thing is when you wake up and there he is, you feel him beside you, and you feel him touching your shoulders. Touching your shoulders with his breath, which is as gentle as the feather of a nightingale.

BRIDE-TO-BE (*fiercely*). I said shut up!

MAID. But listen! What do you think a wedding is? That is all a wedding is. And nothing else. You think it's the canapés? You think it's the flowers? No. It's a bed that glows with a man and woman inside it.

BRIDE-TO-BE. You shouldn't say such things.

MAID. It's something else. Something so full of joy!

BRIDE-TO-BE. Or bitterness.

MAID. Now I'm going to put your garland here, so that it really shows off your hair. (*She tries on her the orange-blossom garland.*)

BRIDE-TO-BE (*looking at herself in the mirror*). Take it off. (*She takes off the garland, looks at it, and bows her head as if defeated.*)

MAID. What are you doing?

BRIDE-TO-BE. Leave me alone.

MAID. This is no time to get sad. (*Trying to cheer her up*). Bring me the garland. (*The* BRIDE-TO-BE *throws it away.*) Don't do that! You'll make something bad happen, throwing your garland onto the floor like that. Lift your head. Look at me. Don't you want to get married? Tell me. It's not too late to turn back. (*She gets up.*)

BRIDE-TO-BE. It's just worries. Clouds. A cold wind in the heart. Doesn't everyone get it?

MAID. You love the man you're going to marry.

BRIDE-TO-BE. I love him.

MAID. Yes, yes, I know you do.

BRIDE-TO-BE. But this is such a big step to take.

MAID. You have to take it.

BRIDE-TO-BE. And I am committed to it.

MAID. I'll fix your veil.

BRIDE-TO-BE (*sitting down*). Hurry up. They'll be here soon.

MAID. They'll still have at least another two hours to go.

BRIDE-TO-BE. How far is it from here to the church?

MAID. Five miles along the riverbed. The road takes twice as long.

The BRIDE-TO-BE *gets up, and the* MAID *becomes excited on seeing her.*

Little bride, little bride, open your eyes
Today is your wedding, quickly arise
The river be strong, the river be wide
To carry the veil to the beautiful bride.

BRIDE-TO-BE (*smiling*). Let's go.

MAID (*kisses her in joy and dances all around her*).
Wake up, wake up, little bride
The trees they are green and in flower outside
The orange tree in blossom
The may tree in flower
They smile in the sunlight
To garnish your bower!

We hear someone knocking on the door.

BRIDE-TO-BE. It must be the first guests. Open the door! (*She goes in.*)

The MAID *opens door and reacts with surprise.*

MAID. You!

LEONARDO. Me. Good morning.

MAID. The first to come!

LEONARDO. Haven't I been invited?

MAID. Yes.

LEONARDO. That's why I've come.

MAID. Where's your wife?

LEONARDO. I came by horse. She's taking the road.

MAID. Didn't you meet anyone?

LEONARDO. I rode past them.

MAID. One day you're going to kill that horse with all that riding.

LEONARDO. When it's dead, it's dead!

Pause.

MAID. Sit down. No one else is up yet.

LEONARDO. Where's the bride-to-be?

MAID. I'm just about to get her dressed.

LEONARDO. About to be married. How happy she'll be.

MAID (*changing the subject*). How's the boy?

LEONARDO. What boy?

MAID. Your son.

LEONARDO (*as if remembering a dream*). Him.

MAID. Are they bringing him?

LEONARDO. No.

Pause. We hear VOICES *singing a long way off.*

VOICES. Little bride, little bride, open your eyes
Today is your wedding, quickly arise

LEONARDO. Little bride, little bride, open your eyes
Today is your wedding, quickly arise

MAID. It's the guests coming. They're still a long way off.

LEONARDO (*getting up*). She'll be wearing a big veil, I imagine. But it shouldn't be that big. A smaller one would suit her better. And has the bridegroom brought the orange blossom she should wear on her breast?

BRIDE-TO-BE (*appearing, still in her petticoats and wearing the orange blossom*). He brought it.

MAID (*fiercely*). Don't come out dressed like that.

BRIDE-TO-BE. What difference does it make? (*Gravely.*) Why did you ask whether they'd brought the orange blossom? What did you mean?

LEONARDO. Nothing. What could I be meaning? (*Coming up to her.*) You know me. You know there's nothing I'm implying. I just want to know something. So tell me. What did I mean to you? Open the chest of your memory. Open it wide. Two oxen and a tiny house are worth almost nothing. But that's all I had. That's where it wounds me.

BRIDE-TO-BE. Why did you come?

LEONARDO. To see you married.

BRIDE-TO-BE. I saw you married too!

LEONARDO. I'm tied to you. You know that. You made the rope. With your own hands. They can kill me, those others, but they've no right to spit on me. All your silver gleams so bright. It spits on people sometimes.

BRIDE-TO-BE. Liar!

LEONARDO. I don't want to speak. I have my pride. I don't want these hills to hear my cries.

BRIDE-TO-BE. My cries would be louder.

MAID. These words must stop. You must not speak of the past. (*The* MAID *looks at the doors; anxiety has seized her.*)

BRIDE-TO-BE. She's right. I shouldn't even look at you. But it burns my soul to have you coming here and spying on my wedding and making insinuations about the orange blossom. Go and wait for your wife at the door.

LEONARDO. Can it really be that you and I cannot speak?

MAID (*raging*). No. No, you cannot speak.

LEONARDO. After I got married I've thought night and day about whose fault it was and every time I think of this I think of another fault that eats the one before. But there's always someone. There's always someone to blame!

BRIDE-TO-BE. A man on his horse knows a lot and can do a lot to squeeze love out of a girl lost in a desert. But I've got my pride. That's why I am getting married. And I will lock myself away with my husband who I have to love more than everything.

LEONARDO. Your pride won't help you. (*He comes closer to her.*)

BRIDE-TO-BE. Don't come near me!

LEONARDO. Do you know the worst thing? The worst thing we can do to ourselves? It's to keep silent. To keep silent and burn. What use was my pride to me and not looking at you and leaving you awake night after night? No use! All it did was fan the flames! And you think that time will cure everything and that walls will cover everything up, but it's not true. It's not true. When you get to the heart of things, you cannot make them disappear!

BRIDE-TO-BE (*trembling*). I can't hear you. I can't bear to hear your voice. It's as if I had drunk a bottle of anis and fallen asleep in a bed of roses. And it pulls me, and I know I am drowning, but I go back. I go back.

MAID (*grabbing* LEONARDO *by the lapels*). You must go now!

LEONARDO. Don't be afraid. It's the last time. The last time I'll ever speak to her.

BRIDE-TO-BE. I know I am mad and I know my breast is rotten, rotten with everything I have to put up with, and yet I still stand here, stand here and hear him. Hear him so quietly and watch him move his hands.

LEONARDO. There could be no peace for me unless I said these things. I got married. You get married now.

MAID (*to* LEONARDO). And she is. She is getting married!

VOICES (*singing closer now*). Little bride, little bride, open your eyes.

BRIDE-TO-BE. Open your eyes! (*She runs out to her room.*)

MAID. The guests have come now. (*To* LEONARDO.) Don't see her again.

LEONARDO. Don't worry. I won't. (*He exits left. Day begins to dawn.*)

GIRL 1 (*coming in*). Little bride, little bride, open your eyes
Today is your wedding, quickly arise
The singers they greet her
With a song on each street.

VOICES. Little bride, little bride, open your eyes.

MAID (*joyfully making a din*). Wake up, wake up, little bride
The trees they are green and in flower outside
The orange tree in blossom
The may tree in flower
They smile in the sunlight
To garnish your bower!

GIRL 2 (*coming in*). Little bride, little bride, open your eyes
With your tresses of gold
And your snow-white blouse

Your boots of patent leather
Jasmine on your brows.

MAID. O beautiful goat girl
By the light of the moon!

GIRL 1. O handsome young shepherd
In the heat of the noon!

BOY 1 (*coming in with his hat in the air*).
Little bride, little bride, open your eyes
For the wedding has woken, the wedding will rise
The wedding is coming through the grass of the fields
To pick the sweet flower that the bride sweetly yields.

VOICES. Little bride, little bride, open your eyes!

GIRL. The bride's crown is all white
And the bridegroom he binds her
With laces of light.

MAID. The bride cannot sleep
In the groves of sweet fruit

GIRL 3 (*coming in*). So the bridegroom he plays her
Sweet notes from his flute.

Three GUESTS *enter*.

BOY 1. Wake bird, white bird!
The dawn she dispels
From the night's blue black darkness
Its shadows deep dark bells.

GUEST. White bride, white bride
A virgin in the morning
A woman by night.

GIRL 1. Come down, you dark beauty
In the silk of your dress

GUEST. Come down, you dark beauty
For the morning dew to bless.

BOY 1. Wake up, lady, wake up
For the orange blossom stirs in the wind.

MAID. I want to plant her a tree
With red ribbons on every branch

A good wish on every ribbon
For happiness and long life.

VOICES. Little bride, little bride, open your eyes.

BOY 1. On the day of your wedding!

GUEST. On the day of your wedding
How lovely you will be
You'll be the flower of the mountains
A captain's bride of the sea.

FATHER (*coming in*). The bridegroom's a captain
Who has come for his bride
He brings priceless treasure
To have by his side.

MAID. Oh, my lovely girl!

BOY 2. Let the bride awaken.

MAID. My beauty!

GIRL 1. The wedding is calling
Through all the windows.

GIRL 2. Let the bride come out.

GIRL 1. Come out, come out!

MAID. Let the bells ring and ring again!

BOY 1. Let her come! Let her come out!

MAID. The wedding is rising, rising like a bull!

The BRIDE-TO-BE *appears. She wears an 1890's black dress, with
hip pads and a long train covered in pleated gauze and intricate lace work.
Her hair falls across her forehead and she wears the orange-blossom
garland. The guitars play. The* GIRLS *kiss the* BRIDE-TO-BE.

GIRL 3. What perfume did you put in your hair?

BRIDE-TO-BE (*laughing*). None.

GIRL 2 (*looking at the dress*). They just don't make silk like that any
more.

BOY 1. Here's the bridegroom!

BRIDEGROOM. Cheers!

GIRL 1 (*putting a flower in his ear*). The bridegroom looks like a golden flower.

GIRL 2. Tears of happiness rising up from his eyes!

The BRIDEGROOM *stands beside the* BRIDE-TO-BE.

BRIDE-TO-BE. Why did you wear those shoes?

BRIDEGROOM. They're cheerier than black ones.

LEONARDO*'s* WIFE *enters.*

WIFE (*kissing the* BRIDE-TO-BE). Good health!

Everyone talks in a loud and lively way.

LEONARDO (*coming in as one who is fulfilling a duty*).
On the morning of the wedding
We greet you.

WIFE. The fields are laughing
At your beauty and your joy!

MOTHER (*to the* FATHER). What are they doing here?

FATHER. They're family. This is a day for forgiveness!

MOTHER. I don't forgive. I put up with it.

BRIDEGROOM. It's so good to see you with your crown on!

BRIDE-TO-BE. Let's go to the church! Quickly!

BRIDEGROOM. Why the hurry?

BRIDE-TO-BE. Because I want to be your wife and be alone with you and hear no other voice but yours.

BRIDEGROOM. That's what I want too!

BRIDE-TO-BE. And see nothing but your eyes. And for you to embrace me with such strength that I could never break free from your arms. Not even if my mother was to call me from beyond the grave.

BRIDEGROOM. My arms are strong. Strong enough to embrace you fifty years.

BRIDE-TO-BE (*fiercely, grabbing him by the arm*). For ever!

FATHER. Time we were going. Pick up the horses and the carts! For the sun has risen.

MOTHER. Take care! Let's not lose the good luck.

The big door at the rear of the stage is opened. People start to leave.

MAID (*crying*). As you leave your house
Virgin all in white
Remember you are leaving
Like a star in the sky . . .

GIRL 1. Clean in your clothes and in your body
Leaving your house to get married.

They keep leaving.

GIRL 2. You are leaving your house for the church!

MAID. On the sands of the desert
Sweet flowers are growing!

GIRL 3. For the lovely girl all white!

MAID. The lace of her mantilla
Is like a dark cloud.

They leave. We hear guitars, castanets and tambourines. LEONARDO
and his WIFE *remain alone.*

WIFE. Let's go.

LEONARDO. Where?

WIFE. To the church. But not on your horse. You're coming with
me.

LEONARDO. In the cart?

WIFE. How else?

LEONARDO. I'm not a man to travel in a cart.

WIFE. And I'm not a woman to go without her husband to a
wedding. I can't take any more.

LEONARDO. Me neither!

WIFE. Why are you looking at me like that? You have a thorn in
each eye.

LEONARDO. Let's go.

WIFE. I don't know what's happening. But I think I know and I
don't want to think. One thing I do know. I've been rejected.
But I have a son. And another child on the way. And life goes

on. The same thing happened to my mother. But this is my place. And I'm not giving way.

VOICES *outside*.

VOICES. As you're leaving your house
    To church in the car
    Remember you're rising
    In the sky like a star.

WIFE (*crying*). Remember you're rising
    In the sky like a star.

That's how I came out of my house too. And the whole countryside belonged to me. It was all mine.

LEONARDO (*getting up*). Let's go.

WIFE. But with me!

LEONARDO. Yes. (*Pause.*) Let's go. (*They leave.*)

VOICES. As you're leaving your house
    To church in the car
    Remember you're rising
    In the sky like a star.

Slow curtain.

Scene Two

Outside the house of the BRIDE-TO-BE. *A landscape of grey whites and cold blues. Large prickly pears. Dark and silvery tones. Views of biscuit-coloured hills. Everything hardened, as if glazed. Like a landscape from traditional pottery.*

MAID (*setting out glasses and trays on a table*).
    The wheel is turning, turning
    And the water is flowing, flowing
    Because the wedding is coming
    The branches are rustling
    And the moon shines like a lover
    On her white veranda.

    (*Loud voice.*) Bring out the tablecloths.

    (*Poetic voice.*) The couple are singing
    And the water is flowing

Because the wedding is coming
The starch of the tablecloths shines like the stars
And let the bitterness of the almonds
Be smothered in sweet honey.

(*Loud voice.*) Get the wine ready!

(*Poetic voice.*) Lovely girl
Lovely girl of the earth
Look how the water is flowing.
Gather in your skirts now your wedding has come
And stay in your house under the bridegroom's wing.
Because the bridegroom's a robin
With his fiery breast
And the countryside is awaiting
The sound of flowing blood.

The wheel is turning
And the water is flowing
Because your wedding has come!

MOTHER (*coming in*). At last!

FATHER. Are we the first?

MAID. No. Leonardo and his wife came in a while ago. They were running like demons. By the time she got here, his wife was half-dead of fright. They made the journey as if they were riding horseback.

FATHER. That man has bad blood. He is out to destroy himself.

MOTHER. What else can you expect? He has the blood of all his family. It comes from his great grandfather, who started off the killing, and it goes on through the whole bad breed – the people with false smiles. The handlers of knives.

FATHER. Let's leave it!

MAID. How can she leave it?

MOTHER. It hurts me to the very pit of my guts. All I can see when I look at them is the stain of my family's blood. Stamped on their forehead like the mark of Cain. You see me? Do I look mad? Well, it was not madness to have screamed as much as my heart needed. In my heart I have a scream, always waiting, a scream I have to discipline and repress and try to smother under blankets. But here I am. In the presence of my dead and I'm supposed to be polite. And people still criticise. (*She removes her cloak.*)

FATHER. This is not a good day to remember these things.

MOTHER. When it comes up in conversation, I have to talk about it. And especially today. Because now I am alone.

FATHER. But expecting company soon.

MOTHER. Yes. That's what I hope for: grandchildren.

They sit.

FATHER. I want them to have a great many. This land needs arms to work it. Arms you don't have to pay. You have to keep up a constant battle with weeds, with thistles, with stones that keep emerging from God knows where. And these arms must belong to the masters, who punish and who dominate, and who make the seeds grow. You need a lot of sons.

MOTHER. And a daughter! Men belong to the wind! Men are forced to wield weapons. Girls don't ever go out on the street.

FATHER (*happily*). I think they'll have plenty of both.

MOTHER. My son will cover her well. He has good seed. His father could have had many sons by me.

FATHER. But I'd want it all to happen in one day. So that immediately they had two or three men.

MOTHER. But that's not how it is. It all takes a long time. That's why it's so terrible to see your own blood spilt on the ground. A fountain that runs for a minute but whose growth has taken us years and years. When I went to see my son, he was lying halfway across the street. I dipped my hands in his blood and I licked them with my tongue. Because it was my blood. You don't understand that. I'd put the earth soaked in his blood in a reliquary made of precious stones.

FATHER. But now you'll just have to wait. My daughter is broad and your son is strong.

MOTHER. That's what I am expecting.

They get up.

FATHER. Prepare the trays of wheat.

MAID. They're already prepared.

LEONARDO's WIFE *enters.*

WIFE. May it be for the good!

MOTHER. Thank you.

LEONARDO. Will there be a party?

FATHER. Not much. Young people these days just don't know how to amuse themselves.

MAID. They've just arrived!

The GUESTS *start arriving in cheerful groups. The newly-weds arrive arm in arm.* LEONARDO *goes.*

BRIDEGROOM. There's never been so many people at a wedding.

BRIDE-TO-BE *(sombrely)*. Never.

FATHER. The ceremony went excellently well.

MOTHER. Whole branches of families have come.

BRIDEGROOM. People who normally don't leave their house.

MOTHER. Your father sowed a lot and now you reap the harvest.

BRIDEGROOM. There were cousins there I had never met before.

MOTHER. Everyone from the coast.

BRIDEGROOM *(cheerfully)*. And they were frightened of the horses!

He talks to the GUESTS.

MOTHER *(to the* BRIDE-TO-BE*)*. What are you thinking about?

BRIDE-TO-BE. Nothing.

MOTHER. The wedding blessings seem to lie heavy.

We can hear guitars.

BRIDE-TO-BE. Like lead.

MOTHER *(fiercely)*. But they should weigh nothing. You should be as light as a dove.

BRIDE-TO-BE. Are you staying here tonight?

MOTHER. No. My house is lonely.

BRIDE-TO-BE. You should stay here!

FATHER (*to the* MOTHER). Look at the dance they are beginning to form. A dance from beyond the shores of the sea.

LEONARDO *enters and sits down. His* WIFE *is behind him, rigid.*

MOTHER. That's my husband's cousins. When it comes to dancing, they are as hard as stones.

FATHER. It makes me happy to see them. What a change for this house! (*He goes.*)

BRIDEGROOM (*to the* BRIDE-TO-BE). Did you like the orange blossom?

BRIDE-TO-BE (*staring at him*). Yes.

BRIDEGROOM. It was all made of wax. I'd like you to have had it all over your dress.

BRIDE-TO-BE. There was no need.

LEONARDO *exits right.*

GIRL 1. We're going to take down your hair.

BRIDE-TO-BE (*to the* BRIDEGROOM). I'll be back in a minute.

WIFE. You be happy. You be happy with my cousin.

BRIDEGROOM. I'm sure I will be.

WIFE. And here you'll be: together. Making up your home. Not going out. I wish I lived as far out as this!

BRIDEGROOM. Why not buy land here? It's cheap on the mountain and the fresh air'll do your children good.

WIFE. We've no money. And the way things are going!

BRIDEGROOM. Your husband's a good worker.

WIFE. Yes, but he never settles. He goes from one thing to the next. Never sticks to anything.

MAID. Aren't you going to take something? Your mother loves these little cakes. I'm wrapping some up for her.

BRIDEGROOM. Give her three dozen.

WIFE. No. Half a dozen will be plenty.

BRIDEGROOM. Today's the day.

WIFE (*to the* MAID). Have you seen Leonardo?

MAID. Never saw him.

BRIDEGROOM. He must be with the others.

WIFE. I'll go and look! (*She goes.*)

MAID. It's all so beautiful.

BRIDEGROOM. Why aren't you dancing?

MAID. There's no one to ask me.

> *Two* GIRLS *walk by upstage; during the whole act there should be a lively crossing of figures back and forth in the background.*

BRIDEGROOM (*cheerfully*). That's terrible! People are so silly! People like you who are old but full of life. You dance better than young people.

MAID. So you're flirting with me. What a family you are! Real men. When I was a girl I was at your grandfather's wedding. What a man! Tall as a mountain.

BRIDEGROOM. I'm not as tall as him.

MAID. But you've the same glint in your eyes. Where's the bride?

BRIDEGROOM. Taking off her veil.

MAID. Ah. Now listen. When it comes to the middle of the night, seeing as how you won't be sleeping, I've put out some ham for you. And some big glasses of good wine. By the larder door. Just in case you need it.

BRIDEGROOM (*smiling*). I never eat at night!

MAID (*maliciously*). If you won't, maybe she will. (*She goes.*)

FIRST YOUNG MAN (*coming in*). Come and have a drink!

BRIDEGROOM. I'm waiting for the bride.

SECOND YOUNG MAN. You'll have her in the morning.

FIRST YOUNG MAN. When you'll enjoy her more.

SECOND YOUNG MAN. Come on. Just for a minute.

BRIDEGROOM. Coming.

They leave. There's a great commotion. The BRIDE *enters. From the other side of the stage come two* GIRLS *running to meet her.*

GIRL 1. Who did you give the first pin to? Was it me? Or was it her?

BRIDE. I can't remember.

GIRL 1. You gave it to me here.

GIRL 2. You gave it to me in the church.

BRIDE (*in great disquiet and in the midst of a profound inner struggle*). I don't know.

GIRL 1. It's just I want to know . . .

BRIDE (*interrupting*). And I don't care! I've got so much to think about . . .

GIRL 2. I'm sorry.

LEONARDO *crosses upstage.*

BRIDE (*seeing* LEONARDO). And this is a difficult time.

GIRL 1. We don't know what it's like!

BRIDE. You'll know when the time comes. This is a step that costs so much.

GIRL 1. Are you unhappy?

BRIDE. No. Forgive me.

GIRL 2. What for? I mean . . . these pins matter. Because they tell when you're going to get married. And it matters, when you get married. Doesn't it?

BRIDE. Yes. Of course it does.

GIRL 1. They mean one of us will get married before the other.

BRIDE. Are you really so keen to get married?

GIRL 2 (*embarrassed*). Yes.

BRIDE. Why?

GIRL 1. Well . . . (*Embracing the second* GIRL.)

The two of them run off. The BRIDEGROOM *appears and, very slowly, embraces the* BRIDE *from behind.*

BRIDE (*in huge alarm*). Get off me!

BRIDEGROOM. Are you afraid of me?

BRIDE. I didn't know it was you.

BRIDEGROOM. Who else could it be? (*Pause.*) Either your father, or me.

BRIDE. Of course.

BRIDEGROOM. Only your father would have embraced you more gently.

BRIDE (*sombrely*). Obviously.

BRIDEGROOM. Because he's old. (*Embraces her fiercely in a way that is a little brusque.*)

BRIDE (*dryly*). Leave me alone!

BRIDEGROOM. Why? (*He lets go of her.*)

BRIDE. It's just . . . all these people. They could see us.

Again, the MAID *crosses upstage. She does not look at the couple.*

BRIDEGROOM. So what? Now we're allowed to.

BRIDE. Yes but leave me . . . Come back later.

BRIDEGROOM. What's the matter? You seem frightened.

BRIDE. It's nothing. Don't leave me.

LEONARDO*'s* WIFE *enters.*

WIFE. I don't want to interrupt . . .

BRIDEGROOM. What is it?

WIFE. Did my husband happen to go by?

BRIDEGROOM. No.

WIFE. I just can't find him. And the horse isn't in the stable.

BRIDEGROOM (*cheerfully*). He must have gone out for a ride.

The WIFE *goes off, anxiously. The* MAID *enters.*

MAID. There's been so many people to congratulate you! You must be so happy.

BRIDEGROOM. I'm hoping all this ends soon. She's a bit tired.

MAID. What's wrong, love?

BRIDE. There's a hammering in my head.

MAID. You have to be strong to get married here in the mountains! (*To the* BRIDEGROOM.) She's yours now. So you're the only one who can make her better. (*She runs off.*)

BRIDEGROOM (*embracing her*). Let's go and have a little dance. (*He kisses her.*)

BRIDE (*in anguish*). No. I'd like to lie down a while.

BRIDEGROOM. I'll keep you company.

BRIDE. You mustn't! With everyone still here? They'd be talking about it for weeks! Just let me rest a moment.

BRIDEGROOM. Whatever you want! But don't be like this tonight!

BRIDE (*at the door*). Tonight I'll be better.

BRIDEGROOM. And that's what I want!

The MOTHER *appears.*

MOTHER. Son.

BRIDEGROOM. What are you up to?

MOTHER. All this to-do. Are you happy?

BRIDEGROOM. Yes.

MOTHER. What about your wife?

BRIDEGROOM. She's having a little rest. It's hard work being a bride!

MOTHER. Hard work? Nonsense. It's the only day of rest. For me it was like coming into an inheritance.

The MAID *enters and heads for the* BRIDE'*s room.*

It's the ploughing of the fields. It's the planting of new trees.

BRIDEGROOM. Are you going to go?

MOTHER. Yes. I must be in my house.

BRIDEGROOM. On your own.

MOTHER. No. Not alone. For my house is full of memories. Full of old struggles. Full of men.

BRIDEGROOM. But these old wars are not wars any more.

The MAID *enters in haste. She runs out the back.*

MOTHER. As long as one lives, one is always at war.

BRIDEGROOM. Advise me. I'll always obey you!

MOTHER. Try to be affectionate with your wife. But if she gets a bit surly or uppish, embrace her in a way that hurts her a little, maybe with a little bite, and then a gentle caress. So she can't get upset or offended, but so she knows you are the man, you are the master, you are the one in command. That's what I learnt from your father. And since you don't have him, I'm the one who has to teach you to be strong.

BRIDEGROOM. I'll always do what you say.

FATHER (*coming in*). Where's my daughter?

BRIDEGROOM. Gone inside.

The FATHER *goes out.*

GIRL 1. Where's the happy couple? We're going to do the wedding dance.

YOUNG MAN 1 (*to the* BRIDEGROOM). You have to lead it.

FATHER (*coming in from the back*). She isn't here!

YOUNG MAN. Isn't she?

FATHER. She must have gone up to the balcony.

BRIDEGROOM. I'll go and see. (*He goes.*)

We hear a bustle, and the playing of guitars.

GIRL 1. They've started already! (*She goes.*)

BRIDEGROOM (*coming in*). She's not there.

MOTHER (*worriedly*). She's not?

FATHER. Where could she have gone?

MAID (*coming in*). But where's the girl?

MOTHER (*gravely*). We don't know.

The BRIDEGROOM *goes out. Three* GUESTS *enter.*

FATHER (*dramatically*). But . . . isn't she in the dance?

MAID. No. She is not in the dance.

FATHER (*emphatically*). There are so many people there. Look!

MAID. I have looked!

FATHER (*tragically*). Then where can she be?

BRIDEGROOM (*coming in*). No sign. She's nowhere to be found.

MOTHER (*to the* FATHER). What is happening? Where is your daughter?

LEONARDO's WIFE *enters*.

WIFE. They've run. They've run! Her and Leonardo! On the horse! Holding each other. As if carried by the wind!

FATHER. Not my daughter! It can't be true!

MOTHER. Yes. Your daughter! The fruit of a bad mother. And him too. Yes, him too. But she is now wife to my son!

BRIDEGROOM (*coming in*). Let's go after them! Who has a horse?

MOTHER. Who has a horse, right now who has a horse? I'd give them everything I have, my eyes and even my tongue . . .

VOICE. There's one here.

MOTHER (*to her son*). After them! Go on!

He goes with two YOUNG MEN.

No. Don't go. These people kill on the spot and then . . . but yes, after them! Run! And I'll follow!

FATHER. It can't be her. Perhaps she went to the well.

MOTHER. Women with honour go to the well. Women who are pure: not your daughter! But now she is my son's wife. Two groups. Here there are two groups.

They all come in.

My family and yours. All of you, get out of here. Shake the dust of this place off your feet. Go help my son.

People separate into two groups.

Because he has people: his cousins from the sea and all those come from inland. Let's go now! Search all the paths. Two bands. You with yours and me with mine. Go now! Go!

Curtain.

ACT THREE

Scene One

A wood. It's night-time. Huge damp trees. A dark atmosphere. We hear two violins.

Three WOODCUTTERS *enter.*

WOODCUTTER 1. Have they found them?

WOODCUTTER 2. Not yet. But they are looking everywhere.

WOODCUTTER 3. They'll find them soon.

WOODCUTTER 2. Ssssshhh!

WOODCUTTER 3. What?

WOODCUTTER 2. They are getting closer.

WOODCUTTER 1. They'll see them when the moon rises.

WOODCUTTER 2. They should let them be.

WOODCUTTER 1. The world is wide. There's room for everyone to live in it.

WOODCUTTER 3. But they'll kill them.

WOODCUTTER 2. They were right to run away. You have to follow your heart's deep feeling.

WOODCUTTER 1. They were each deceiving the other, and in the end the blood was stronger.

WOODCUTTER 3. Blood.

WOODCUTTER 1. You have to follow the path of blood.

WOODCUTTER 2. But when blood sees the light of day, the earth swallows it.

WOODCUTTER 1. So what? Better to bleed to death than live with it putrid.

WOODCUTTER 3. Be quiet.

WOODCUTTER 1. Why? Do you hear anything?

WOODCUTTER 3. I hear the crickets. I hear the toads. I hear the night watching.

WOODCUTTER 1. But there's no sign of the horse.

WOODCUTTER 3. No.

WOODCUTTER 1. Just now they'll be making love.

WOODCUTTER 2. Her body his. His body hers.

WOODCUTTER 3. They'll seek them out and they'll kill them.

WOODCUTTER 1. But by then they will have mingled their blood and they will be like two empty jars or two dried-up streams.

WOODCUTTER 2. There are so many clouds. It would be easy for the moon to hide.

WOODCUTTER 3. With the moon, or without the moon. It makes no difference. The bridegroom will find them. I saw him leave. Like an angry star. His face the colour of ash. He personified the destiny of his caste.

WOODCUTTER 1. His caste of corpses lying in the street.

WOODCUTTER 2. That's right.

WOODCUTTER 3. Do you think they'll break out of the circle?

WOODCUTTER 2. Unlikely. There are rifles and knives for ten leagues all around.

WOODCUTTER 1. He rides a good horse.

WOODCUTTER 2. But he carries a woman.

WOODCUTTER 1. We are close now.

WOODCUTTER 2. Look. A tree of forty branches. Soon we'll have it felled.

WOODCUTTER 3. Let's make haste. The moon is rising.

There is a lightness rising on the left.

WOODCUTTER 1. The rising moon!
Moon of the large leaves.

WOODCUTTER 2. Fill the blood with jasmine!

WOODCUTTER 1. The lonely moon!
Moon of leaves of green!

WOODCUTTER 2. Silver on the face of the bride.

WOODCUTTER 3. The wicked moon!
Leave the branch dark for love.

WOODCUTTER 1. The sad moon!
Leave the branch for love to hide in.

They leave. The MOON *enters through the lightening on the left. The* MOON *is a young woodcutter with a white face. The stage becomes a vivid tone of blue.*

MOON. My light glitters in the water like a swan
In the night sky like the implacable eye of God
And on the leaves I shine a false dawn.
So no. They'll not escape, they can't.
Is there anyone trying to hide
Anyone sobbing like a broken heart?
The moon has left in the air
A knife with a blade of lead
An ambush to make grief in the blood.
It's so cold outside windows and walls!
Let me in! So I can warm me!
Open the chests of the grave clothes
For only they can keep me warm.
I am cold! I am the ash of burnt-out fires
Seeking a spark in the warm bodies
Sleeping in the streets and fields.
I am carried on the shoulders of snowdrifts
And glint dully in the hard cold water of ditches and ponds.
And today red blood will warm my frozen cheeks
So I don't want any shadow I don't want any hiding place
Where they can evade or escape me.
I want to creep into a gaping wound and warm me!
Let me in, o let me in!

To the branches.

I don't want shadows.
I want my rays to penetrate every darkness
So that among the shadows of the trees
There is a rumour of clarity
So that tonight my cheeks may take their fill of sweet blood.
Who is hiding? Winkle them out!
Make sure they cannot escape!

He disappears among the tree trunks, and the stage returns to its state of dark light. An old BEGGARWOMAN *enters, completely covered by dark green rags. Her feet are naked. It is hard to see her face amongst the folds of her costume. This character must not be listed in the programme.*

BEGGARWOMAN.
The moon has gone. They are coming nearer.
They will get no further.
It has to be here. It has to be now. I am tired.
They have opened the funeral trunks, and the grave clothes
Are awaiting on the alcove floor
For the heavy corpses with their wounds gaping.
I don't want a single bird to cry.
I want the wind to gather up the screams
And run with them past the black treetops
And bury them under the river's soft slime.

(*Impatiently.*) Where is that moon?

The MOON *appears. The intense blue light reappears.*

MOON. Now they're getting closer.
Some by the river and some by the ravine.
I'm going to make the stones gleam.
What do you need?

BEGGARWOMAN. Nothing.

MOON. The air bites harshly. With a double blade.

BEGGARWOMAN.
I want light in their clothes. I want the buttons open.
I want the knives to know the way in.

MOON. I want them to take a long time dying.
I want the blood running through my fingers to make
a delicate sound.

BEGGARWOMAN. Let's not allow them past. Silence!

MOON. Here they come!

He goes. The stage is left in darkness.

BEGGARWOMAN. Hurry! Light! Have you heard me?
I don't want them to escape!

The BRIDEGROOM *and* YOUNG MAN 1 *enter. The* BEGGARWOMAN *sits down and covers herself with her cloak.*

BRIDEGROOM. This way.

YOUNG MAN 1. You'll never find them.

BRIDEGROOM (*fiercely*). I will!

YOUNG MAN 1. I think they took another path.

BRIDEGROOM. No. I heard horse's hooves a moment ago.

YOUNG MAN 1. Most likely another horse.

BRIDEGROOM (*with fierce emotion*). Listen. There is only one horse in the world. And that horse is the one. You understand me? If you're going to follow me, just follow. Don't speak.

YOUNG MAN 1. It's just I wanted . . .

BRIDEGROOM. Silence. I am sure I will find them here. See this arm? It is no longer mine. It's my brother's and my father's and every member of my family that's been killed. It is so strong, if it wanted it could tear out that tree by the roots. Let's go now. I can feel the ghosts of all my family crowd around me so I cannot breathe easily.

The BEGGARWOMAN *moans with pain.*

YOUNG MAN 1. Did you hear that?

BRIDEGROOM. Take that path and work your way round.

YOUNG MAN 1. We're on a hunt.

BRIDEGROOM. The greatest hunt that can ever be.

The YOUNG MAN *goes. The* BRIDEGROOM *heads rapidly to the left and trips over the* BEGGARWOMAN. *Over* DEATH.

BEGGARWOMAN. Ay!

BRIDEGROOM. What do you want?

BEGGARWOMAN. I am cold.

BRIDEGROOM. Where are you heading?

BEGGARWOMAN. Far over there . . .

BRIDEGROOM. Where have you come from?

BEGGARWOMAN. From a long way off.

BRIDEGROOM. Did you see a man and a woman running away on a horse?

BEGGARWOMAN (*as if waking*). Wait . . . (*Looking at him.*) What a beautiful young man. (*She gets up.*) But even lovelier were he sleeping.

BRIDEGROOM. Did you see them?

BEGGARWOMAN. Wait. What broad shoulders you have. How heavy they must be. They're crushing your delicate feet. Wouldn't you be better off resting them on the ground?

BRIDEGROOM (*shaking her*). I asked you if you saw them! Have they been this way?

BEGGARWOMAN (*fiercely*). No, they've not been. They're just coming down the hill. Can't you hear them?

BRIDEGROOM. No.

BEGGARWOMAN. Don't you know the way?

BRIDEGROOM. I'll go any way I can!

BEGGARWOMAN. I'll come with you. This earth, this place. I know them well.

BRIDEGROOM (*impatiently*). Come on then! But where?

BEGGARWOMAN. Over there!

They make a quick exit. A long way off we hear two violins. They are the wood. The WOODCUTTERS *return. They carry axes on their shoulders. They pass slowly between the trees.*

WOODCUTTER 1. Death is rising!
Death of the large leaves.

WOODCUTTER 2. Don't open the torrent of blood!

WOODCUTTER 1. The lonely death.
Death of the dry leaves.

WOODCUTTER 3. Don't cover the wedding with funeral flowers.

WOODCUTTER 2. O sad death.
Leave the green branch for love.

WOODCUTTER 1. O sad death!
Leave for love the branch of green.

They leave as they talk. LEONARDO *and the* BRIDE *enter.*

LEONARDO. Quiet!

BRIDE. I want you to go back. Go!
From now on I'll go alone.

LEONARDO. I said be quiet!

BRIDE. I used to have self-respect.
Now there's a chain around my neck.
Take it off, if you can,
With your hands, if you can,
With your teeth, if you must.
And then leave me
In a corner of my house, on my earth.
Or maybe you want to kill me
Like you'd kill a poisonous snake
Give me the gun, place it in my hands
In the hands of this person who once was a bride.
There's fire burning in my head.
There's an ocean drowning my heart.
My tongue is pegged down with shards of glass.

LEONARDO. We took the first step. Now be quiet!
They're close behind us.
And I will take you away with me.

BRIDE. Then you'll have to do it by force!

LEONARDO. By force?
Who was the first to come down the stairs?

BRIDE. I was.

LEONARDO. Who put a new saddle on the horse?

BRIDE. I did. It's true.

LEONARDO. And whose hands buckled on my spurs?

BRIDE. Yes, my hands, which are your hands now.
Hands which when they see you
Would willingly break the blue branches
And the murmur of your veins.
I love you. I love you. Go!
Because if I could I would kill you
And wrap you in a shroud

Between rows of violets.
There's fire burning in my head.
There's an ocean drowning my heart.

LEONARDO.
My tongue is pegged down with shards of glass.
But I wanted to forget
And I divided my house from yours
With a wall of stone.
It's true. Don't you remember?
And when I saw you from far off
I threw sand into my own eyes.
But whenever I rode my horse
My horse led me to your door.
Silver needles invaded my bloodstream
And turned it black,
And whenever I slept I dreamed
Dreams that filled my flesh with poisoned weeds.
For it's not my fault
It's the fault of the earth
And of the scent exuded by your breasts
That is exhaled by your hair.

BRIDE. Oh, this is such madness!
I don't want to sleep with you
I don't even want to eat with you
Yet there's not a moment of any day
I don't want to be there with you.
Because you drag me along
And when you say 'Go!'
I go
And when you say 'Come!'
I come
I'm like a blade of grass blown about by the wind
And you are the wind that blows me.
You made me leave a hard man.
You made me turn my back on all his family.
At my own wedding you made me abandon him.
At my own wedding, and I was wearing my bride's dress
     and veil.
And you're the one that'll suffer
And I don't want you to

I don't want you to suffer.
Leave me! Run away! Run!
For there's no one who'll defend you.

LEONARDO. The birds of the dawn
Are breaking on the trees
And night is dying
On the hard edge of gravestones.
Let's go to a dark corner
Where I'll always be able to love you
And people won't matter
Nor the poison they throw at us.

He embraces her fiercely.

BRIDE. I'll sleep at your feet.
I'll be the dog that lies at your feet
And watches over everything you're dreaming.
I'll be there naked
And I'll be looking out over the fields.
For when I look at you
When I look at you
Your beauty's a flame
A fierce flame that burns me.

LEONARDO. One flame burns another
And the same small spark
Can burn up two blades of grass
That stand together.

Let's go!

He pulls her after him.

BRIDE. Where are you taking me?

LEONARDO.
Somewhere where those men who are pursuing us
Will never ever find us.
Somewhere where I can look at you!

BRIDE (*sarcastically*). You can take me from fair to fair
And display me as a warning to respectable women.

LEONARDO. If I thought the way everyone thinks
I would want to leave you too.
But I go where you go.

You too. Take a step. Try.
The moon nails your thighs to my waist.

The whole scene is violent and filled with great sensuality.

BRIDE. Do you hear?

LEONARDO. There are people coming.

BRIDE. You run! It's only right that I should die here
With a crown of thorns on my head
And my feet in the river.
And then let the leaves mourn me
For a lost woman and a virgin.

LEONARDO. Quiet. They're coming.

BRIDE. Go!

LEONARDO. Hush. They'll hear us.
You first. I said, Go!

The BRIDE *hesitates.*

BRIDE. Both together!

LEONARDO (*embracing her*). As you wish!
If they separate us, it'll be
Because they've killed me.

BRIDE. And because I'm dead.

They leave, embracing each other.

The MOON *enters very slowly. The stage is lit by a strong blue light.
We hear two violins. Suddenly we hear two piercing screams. The violin
music is cut off. On the second scream the* BEGGARWOMAN
*appears and remains with her back to the audience. She opens her cloak
and stays centrestage like a huge bird with outspread wings. The*
MOON *stands absolutely still. The curtain goes down in total silence.*

Final Scene

*A room in white with thick walls and arches. Stage left and right, two white
staircases. A big arch at the back and a wall of white. Floor in shining white
also. This is a simple room which has the monumental feel of a church.
There will be neither grey, nor shadow, nor even enough to establish a
perspective.*

Two GIRLS *dressed in dark blue are winding a skein of red wool. The* YOUNG GIRL *is also onstage.*

GIRL 1. Thread of life, thread of life
　　What is it you're wanting?

GIRL 2. A dress of white jasmine
　　A paper of glass
　　To be born in the morning
　　To die late at night
　　To be a thread that connects
　　A chain that binds
　　And a knot that ties
　　A crown of bitterness.

YOUNG GIRL (*singing*). Did you go to the wedding?

GIRL 1. No.

YOUNG GIRL. Me neither.
　　What will happen
　　When they come to trim the vines?
　　What will happen
　　When they come to prune the olive trees?
　　Why did no one come back?
　　Did you go to the wedding?

GIRL 2. We told you no.

YOUNG GIRL (*going*). I never went neither.

GIRL 2. Thread of life, thread of life
　　What is it you're singing?

GIRL 1. The wounds are of wax
　　The myrtle is weeping.
　　The morning's for sleeping
　　The night for waking.

YOUNG GIRL (*at the door*). The thread pauses
　　At the threshold of the door.
　　The blue mountains
　　Let it pass.
　　Run, let it run
　　In the end it'll reach
　　The blade of the knife.

　　She goes.

GIRL 2. Thread of life, thread of life
    What is it you're saying?

GIRL 1. A lover without speech
    A lover bathed in blood.
    I saw the two corpses
    By the silent river.

She stops. She looks at the wool.

YOUNG GIRL. Let the red wool run
    Run from her to the door.
    I feel them coming
    Covered with earth.
    Laid-out corpses
    On marble shrouds.

She goes.

    LEONARDO's WIFE *and* MOTHER-IN-LAW *enter. They are full of anguish.*

GIRL 1. Are they coming?

MOTHER-IN-LAW (*bitterly*). We don't know.

GIRL 2. What happened at the wedding?

GIRL 1. Tell us.

MOTHER-IN-LAW (*dryly*). Nothing.

WIFE. I want to go back. I want to know everything.

MOTHER-IN-LAW (*with authority*). You go to your house.
    You will be alone there.
    You will grow old weeping.
    Behind a door that stays closed.
    No one enters. Not the living, not the dead.
    We nail the windows shut.
    Nights pass. Rain falls
    On the bitter herbs.

WIFE. What could have happened?

MOTHER-IN-LAW. Nothing. Cover your face.
    Your sons are your sons.
    That is all.
    Where her pillow was

On the bed
Put a cross of cold ash.

They leave.

BEGGARWOMAN (*at the door*). Girls, give us some bread.

GIRL 1. Go!

The GIRLS *cluster together.*

BEGGARWOMAN. Why?

GIRL 2. Your voice is ugly. Go.

GIRL 1. Girl!

BEGGARWOMAN. I could have asked for your eyes.
Behind me is a flock of birds.
Do you want one?

GIRL 1. I want to go.

GIRL 2. Don't take any notice!

GIRL 1. Did you come by the valley path?

BEGGARWOMAN. That's how I came.

GIRL 1 (*timidly*). May I ask . . . ?

BEGGARWOMAN. I saw them; they came very soon;
Two torrents quiet at last among the large boulders
Two men on the horse's hooves
Dead in the beauty of the night.
(*With fierce delight.*) Dead, yes. Dead.

GIRL 1. Be quiet, old woman.

BEGGARWOMAN. Their eyes are broken flowers
And their teeth two fistfuls of frozen snow.
They both fell, and the bride returns
With blood staining her skirt and her hair.
Two blankets cover them. They are coming
On the shoulders of the tall young men.
That's how it was. It had to be.
Dirty sand on the flower of gold.

She goes. The GIRLS *lower their heads and rhythmically begin to leave.*

GIRL 1. Dirty sand.

GIRL 2. On the flower of gold.

GIRL 1. On the flower of gold
    They carry the dead of the riverbed
    One's hair is brown
    And so is the other's
    What nightingale of shadow
    Swoops and soars
    Above the flower of gold!

She goes. The stage is empty. The MOTHER *appears with a*
NEIGHBOUR. *The* NEIGHBOUR *is crying.*

MOTHER. Stop it.

NEIGHBOUR. I can't.

MOTHER. I said stop it. (*At the door.*) Is no one here? (*She takes her*
hands to her forehead.) My son should be answering. But my son is
now just a handful of withered flowers. My son is now a dark
voice behind the mountains. (*Angrily, to the* NEIGHBOUR.) I
said stop it! I don't want crying in this house. Your tears just
come from your eyes. Mine will come when I am alone. Come
from the soles of my feet, from my roots in the earth. And they
will burn more fiercely than blood.

NEIGHBOUR. Don't stay here. Come to my house.

MOTHER. Here. This is where I want to be. At rest. They're all
dead now. I'll sleep at midnight, I'll sleep without being
frightened by the rifle or the knife. When the rain lashes
against the windows, other mothers will run to them to see the
faces of their sons. I won't. I will make out of my dreams a
cold marble dove which carries starched camellias to the
graveyard. But no, not a graveyard: a bed of earth, a bed that
shelters them and cradles them in the sky.

A WOMAN *in black enters and heads to the right and kneels there.*

(*To the* NEIGHBOUR.) Take your hands away from your face.
We will have to live through terrible days. I don't want to see
anyone. The earth and I. My grief and I. And these four walls.
(*She sits, overwhelmed.*)

NEIGHBOUR. Have pity on yourself.

MOTHER (*throwing her head back*). I must be serene. (*She sits.*)

Because the neighbours will be coming and I don't want them to see me so poor. So poor. A woman who doesn't even have a son to carry to her lips.

The BRIDE *appears. She comes without orange blossom and with a black cloak.*

NEIGHBOUR (*seeing the* BRIDE *and asking in fury*). Where are you going?

BRIDE. I'm coming here.

MOTHER (*to the* NEIGHBOUR). Who is that?

NEIGHBOUR. Don't you recognise her?

MOTHER. That's why I ask who she is. I must not recognise her, otherwise I will sink my teeth into her neck. Viper.

She makes for the BRIDE *in fury but suddenly stops.*

(*To the* NEIGHBOUR.) Do you see her? There she is and she's crying and I stay calm and do not claw out her eyes. I don't understand myself. Could it be I never loved my son? But his honour? Where is her honour?

She repeatedly hits the BRIDE, *who falls to the floor.*

NEIGHBOUR. For the love of God! (*She tries to separate them.*)

BRIDE (*to the* NEIGHBOUR). Let her be. I came here so she could kill me and they could carry me with them. (*To the* MOTHER.) But not with your hands: with wire hooks, with a harrow, with a spade, until my bones break. Let her be! Because I want her to know that I am clean, that I may be mad, but that they can bury me without any man having seen the whiteness of my breasts.

MOTHER. Be quiet, be quiet, what does this matter to me?

BRIDE. Because I went with the other one, I went! (*Full of anguish.*) You would have gone too. I was a burnt woman, full of wounds inside and out, and your son was a little drop of water from whom I expected sons, land and health; but the other was a dark river, full of branches, who brought to me the sound of his rushes and the singing between his teeth. And I was running with your son who was like a little boy of cold water, and the other kept sending me great flocks of white doves which stopped me walking and left scorch marks on my wounds, the wounds of a poor lost woman, of a girl caressed by fire. I never loved – listen to me! I never loved him. Your son was my goal and I never deceived him, but the arm of the other dragged me on like waves of the sea and would have dragged me always always always even though I had been an old woman and all the sons of your son dragged me back by the hair!

A NEIGHBOUR *enters.*

MOTHER. Oh no, she's not to blame! (*Sarcastically.*) Whose fault is it then? What kind of woman will throw away her bridal wreath in exchange for a piece of bed another woman has already warmed? Such a weak, delicate princess to sleep so badly at night!

BRIDE. Be quiet! Take your revenge. That's why I'm here. See how soft my neck is; it'll be easier than pruning a flower in your garden. But no! I am honourable, as honourable as a newborn child. And strong enough to prove it. Light a fire. We'll put our hands in the flame: you for your son, me for my honour. And you'll take yours out first.

Another NEIGHBOUR *enters.*

MOTHER. Why should I care about your honour? Why should I care about your death? What does any of this matter? Blessed be the corn, because my sons are under it; blessed be the rain, because it moistens the face of the dead. Blessed be God, who will lay us out to rest.

Another NEIGHBOUR *enters.*

BRIDE. Let me weep with you.

MOTHER. Weep. But at the door.

The YOUNG GIRL *enters. The* BRIDE *stays at the door. The* MOTHER *is centrestage.*

WIFE (*coming in and going to the left*).
He was a beautiful horseman
And now a heap of snow.
He rode through fairs and mountains
On woman's arms.

Now his head is crowned
With night's dank moss.

MOTHER. Sunflower of your mother
Mirror of the earth.
Let them cover your breast
With a cross of bitter oleanders;
A sheet which covers you
With shining silk,
And may water mourn you
Between your quiet hands.

WIFE. Ay, four young men are coming
And their shoulders are weary!

BRIDE. Ay, four handsome young men
Carrying death through the air!

MOTHER. Neighbours.

YOUNG GIRL (*at the door*). They're bringing them now.

MOTHER. It's the same.
The cross, the cross.

WOMEN. Sweet nails
Sweet cross
Sweet name of Jesus.

BRIDE. May the cross protect the living and the dead.

MOTHER. Neighbours: with a knife
With a little knife
On a signalled day, between two and three,
Two men killed each other out of love.
With a knife
Just a little knife
That barely covers the palm of a hand
But which subtly penetrates
Through the startled flesh
And which stops in the place
Where there trembles all tangled
The dark root of a scream.

BRIDE. And this is a knife
Just a little knife
That hardly covers the palm of the hand;

Fish without scales or river
But on one particular day, between two and three
With this knife
Two hard men ended up
With yellow lips.

MOTHER. And which hardly fits in the hand
But which coldly penetrates
The astonished flesh
And there it stops in the place
Where there trembles all tangled
The dark root of a scream.

The NEIGHBOURS, *on their knees on the floor, cry.*

Curtain.

YERMA

(Barren)

*A Tragic Poem in Three Acts
and Six Scenes*

*To
Marni Robertson
another fierce woman of courage*

J.C.

Characters

(in order of appearance)

YERMA
SHEPHERD
BOY CHILD
JUAN
MARIA
VICTOR
PAGAN OLD WOMAN
GIRL 1
GIRL 2
WASHERWOMAN 1
WASHERWOMAN 2
WASHERWOMAN 3
WASHERWOMAN 4
WASHERWOMAN 5
WASHERWOMAN 6
SISTER 1
SISTER 2
DOLORES
OLD WOMAN 1
OLD WOMAN 2
WOMAN 1
WOMAN 2
VILLAGE GIRLS
MALE MASK
FEMALE MASK
BOY
MAN 1
MAN 2

WOMEN, GIRLS, A CROWD

ACT ONE

Scene One

As the curtain rises, we see YERMA *asleep with a sewing basket at her feet.*

The stage is strangely lit, as if in a dream. A SHEPHERD *enters on tiptoe and stares at* YERMA. *He holds the hand of a* BOY CHILD *dressed in white. The clock strikes.*

As the SHEPHERD *leaves the stage, the blue light of the dream transforms into the happy daylight of a spring morning.* YERMA *wakes up.*

SONG (*from within*).
  Rock-a-bye baby
  Let's go and hide
  In a tiny wee housey
  Where we'll shelter inside.

YERMA. Juan. Can you hear me? Juan.

JUAN. Coming.

YERMA. It's time.

JUAN. Have they let out the goats?

YERMA. Yes.

JUAN. See you later. (*About to go.*)

YERMA. Won't you have some milk?

JUAN. Milk?

YERMA. You work so hard and it wears you out.

JUAN. Men have to work hard. That's how we get to be strong. Strong as iron.

YERMA. Yes. But not you. You weren't like this when we married. Now you're so pale. As if the sun never touched you. I wish you'd go down to the river and swim. Or climb onto the roof when the rain falls. Two years we've been married and every day you look worse. More dried up and withered. As if you were shrinking.

JUAN. Finished?

YERMA (*getting up*). Don't be offended. If I was ill I'd love you to look after me. I'd love you to say: 'My wife's ill. I'm going to kill a lamb to make her a nice meat stew.' Or: 'My wife's ill. I'm making up a tub of goose fat to rub on her chest. It'll help her feel better.' 'I'm going to take her a sheepskin to keep her feet warm.' That's how I am. And that's why I want to take care of you.

JUAN. And I thank you.

YERMA. But you won't let yourself be looked after.

JUAN. Why should I? There's nothing wrong with me. You just imagine things. I work hard. That's all there is to it. And each year I get a little older.

YERMA. Yes. Each year . . . and you and me, we carry on year after year . . .

JUAN (*smiling*). Of course we do. And we're doing well. The farm's really making money. And we don't have the expense of children.

YERMA. No. No, we don't have children . . . Juan!

JUAN. What?

YERMA. Is it because I don't love you?

JUAN. No. I know you love me.

YERMA. I know girls who were shaking all over before they went to bed with their husbands and who cried and cried. And did I cry before I went before I went to bed with you? No I did not. And when I slipped in between our fine linen sheets I sang for joy. And didn't I say: 'The bedclothes smell fresh as apples?'

JUAN. That's what you said!

YERMA. I wasn't sorry to leave my mother and that made her cry. It was true. No one was happier than me to get married. But still . . .

JUAN. Don't say it. I've got enough on my hands without having to listen to them saying . . .

YERMA. Don't tell me what they're saying. And I know it's not true. The rain falls on the stones, it falls and it falls, and they become soft earth and a place where the gillyflower grow. And people say they're no use to anybody but I can see their yellow flowers dancing in the sunshine.

JUAN. We have to be patient.

YERMA. Yes. Patient. And loving too!

>*YERMA embraces her husband and kisses him. She takes the lead.*

JUAN. If you need anything just tell me. I'll bring it you. You know I don't like you going out.

YERMA. I never go out.

JUAN. You're better off at home.

YERMA. I know.

JUAN. The street is for people with nothing better to do.

YERMA (*sombrely*). Obviously.

>*The husband leaves.* YERMA *goes to her sewing basket. She passes her hand over her belly, lets out a lovely yawn as she lifts her arms to the sky. And sits down to sew.*

Where are you, my baby, my dear one?
On the slope of the cold cold hill
What are you needing my baby, my dear one?
To cuddle your dress with its frill.

She threads her needle.

The tree waves its branches in the sun
The fountain's clear water does run, does run.

As if she was talking to a child:

The dog barks in the doorway
The wind sings in the trees
The sheep baa to their shepherd
My hair waves up to the moon.
What do you want, my baby forlorn?

Pause.

'I want the white mountains, I want your white breasts'
The tree waves its branches in the sun
The fountain's clear water does run, does run.

Sewing.

I'll say yes to you, my baby, my loved one
Though for you I've been battered and broken
Here in my womb it hurts me, my dear one
My baby, where your first cradle will be.
When will you come, my loved one, come to me, come
    to me?

Pause.

'When your skin smells of the white jasmine tree'
The tree waves its branches in the sun
The fountain's clear water does run, does run.

YERMA *keeps singing.* MARIA *enters through the door, carrying a parcel of clothes.*

YERMA. Where have you been?

MARIA. The shop.

YERMA. So early?

MARIA. I wanted to camp out on the street till opening time! Guess what I've been buying!

YERMA. Coffee, butter, sugar, bread . . .

MARIA. No. Not that. I've been buying material, ribbons, bits of lace, coloured wool to make those fancy bobbles . . . My husband had the money and gave it me himself.

YERMA. You're going to make a blouse.

MARIA. No. Can't you guess?

YERMA. No.

MARIA. It's because . . . He's coming . . . (*She's silent a moment, and hides her face.*)

YERMA *gets up and looks at her admiringly.*

YERMA. After only five months!

MARIA. Yes.

YERMA. And you knew?

MARIA. Of course I did.

YERMA. And how did you know? What did it feel like?

MARIA. I don't know. (*Pause.*) It felt bad.

YERMA. It felt bad. (*Clinging onto her.*) But . . . when did he come? Tell me . . . Maybe you were thinking of something else . . .

MARIA. Yes. Thinking of something else . . .

YERMA. You were singing, maybe? I'm always singing. What about you? Tell me.

MARIA. Don't ask me. Have you ever held a little bird cupped in your hand?

YERMA. Yes.

MARIA. Well, it's like that . . . only it's inside. In your blood.

YERMA. How beautiful! (*She looks at her in wonder.*)

MARIA. I don't know.

YERMA. Don't know what?

MARIA. Don't know what to do. I'll ask my mother.

YERMA. Why ask her? She's old and she'll have forgotten all about it. Don't overdo things and when you breathe, breathe really gently as if in your mouth you were holding a rose.

MARIA. You know something? They say that when he gets a bit bigger he'll start giving me little pushes with his feet.

YERMA. And that's when you love him more than ever. That's when you say: he's my son!

MARIA. And on top of everything I feel really embarrassed.

YERMA. What does your husband say?

MARIA. Nothing.

YERMA. Does he love you?

MARIA. He never says so, but when he comes close to me his eyes kind of shiver like two green leaves.

YERMA. And did he know that you . . . ?

MARIA. Yes.

YERMA. How did he know?

MARIA. I don't know. But that first night we were married he kept telling me, with his mouth next to my cheek, so it seems to me that my son is a dove of light that he poured into my ear.

YERMA. You're so lucky!

MARIA. But you know more about this than I do.

YERMA. And what's the use of it?

MARIA. It's a shame! And why should that be? Of all the girls who got married when you did you're the only one . . .

YERMA. That's just how it is. Obviously there's still time. It took Elena three years, and then there were other girls in my mother's day who took much longer, but to have to wait two years and twenty days like me is just too long. It's not right. I shouldn't have to burn myself up like this. Often I go out the door barefoot just so I can tread the earth. I don't know why. If this goes on like this, I'm going to make myself ill.

MARIA. Oh, come here, love! You're talking like you were old. And you're not! There's no point worrying about these things. One of my mum's sisters had her first when she was forty, and you should have seen what a lovely boy!

YERMA (*with anxious longing*). What was he like?

MARIA. He used to yell like a little bull, so loud he deafened us. And then he peed on us. And he pulled our hair, and when he was four months old he covered our faces with scratches.

YERMA (*laughing*). Things like that don't hurt.

MARIA. Well . . .

YERMA. No they don't! I once saw my sister breast-feeding her baby and her breast was all cracked and sore and it really hurt her. But it was good pain. It was full of life. She needed it to get better.

MARIA. They do say that your children make you suffer.

YERMA. That's not true. It's only weak and whiny mothers say things like that. Why do they have children anyway? Having a son is not like having a bunch of flowers. We have to suffer to see them grow. I think they drink up half our blood. But that's good, healthy, beautiful. Every woman's got enough blood for four or five sons. And when they don't have them this blood turns bad. Like mine.

MARIA. I don't know what's wrong with me.

YERMA. I've heard that first-time mothers get easily scared.

MARIA (*shyly*). Maybe . . . But listen, I was wondering, since you're so good at sewing . . .

YERMA (*taking the bundle*). Fine. I'll cut out his baby clothes. What's in this?

MARIA. That's for his nappies.

YERMA. Good. (*She sits down.*)

MARIA. Thank you. See you soon.

She goes up to YERMA, *who lovingly places her hands on her belly.*

YERMA. Be careful on the cobblestones in the street.

MARIA. Goodbye. (*She kisses her, and goes out.*)

YERMA. Come back soon!

YERMA *is in the same position as she was at the beginning. She picks up her scissors and starts to cut the material. Enter* VICTOR.

Good morning, Victor.

VICTOR (*a man of depth and gravity*). Where's Juan?

YERMA. In the fields.

VICTOR. What are you sewing?

YERMA. Some nappies.

VICTOR (*smiling*). Fancy that.

YERMA (*laughing*). I'm going to edge them with lacework.

VICTOR. If it's a girl you'll give her your name.

YERMA (*trembling*). What?

VICTOR. I'm happy for you.

YERMA (*as if suffocating with her feeling*). No . . . no, they're not for me. They're for Maria's son.

VICTOR. Well, maybe she'll set you a good example! This house needs a child.

YERMA (*with anguish*). Yes. That is what this house needs.

VICTOR. So. Keep trying. Tell your husband not to be so concerned with work. He wants to get money and he'll get it all right, but who will he leave it to? I'm taking my sheep out to pasture. Tell Juan to pick up the two he bought from me. And as for the other thing . . . Tell him to dig deep! (*He goes out smiling.*)

YERMA (*with passion*). Exactly! Tell him to dig deep!

> YERMA *gets up thoughtfully and goes to the spot where* VICTOR *has been. She breathes in deep, as if breathing in fresh air from the mountain. Then she goes to the other side of the room, as if she's looking for something, and from there she goes back to her seat and picks up her sewing. She starts to sew with her eyes fixed on the same point.*

I'll say yes to you, my baby, my loved one
Though for you I've been battered and broken
Here in my womb it hurts me, my dear one
My baby, where your first cradle will be.
When will you come, my loved one, come to me,
　　come to me?
'When your skin smells of the white jasmine tree.'

Curtain.

Scene Two

In the fields. Enter YERMA. *She carries a basket.*

Enter the PAGAN OLD WOMAN.

YERMA. Good morning.

OLD WOMAN. Good morning, my lovely. Where are you off to?

YERMA. I've just taken my husband his midday meal . . . He's working in the field.

OLD WOMAN. You been married long?

YERMA. Three years.

OLD WOMAN. Got any children?

YERMA. No.

OLD WOMAN. Oh well. You will.

YERMA (*with deep anxiety*). You really think so?

OLD WOMAN. Why ever not? (*She sits down.*) I've just taken my husband his dinner too. He's old. Still working. I've got nine sons like sunbeams. But because they're all male, here's me still working like a donkey.

YERMA. You live the other side of the river.

OLD WOMAN. That's me. By the water mill. Who's your family?

YERMA. I'm Enrique the shepherd's daughter.

OLD WOMAN. Ah. Enrique the shepherd. I knew him. Good people. The kind that get up, work hard, eat their daily bread and die. No days off, no days out, nothing. Fiestas are for other people. Never them. Silent creatures. I could have married one of your uncles. But no. He wasn't for me. My skirts swing in the wind. My mouth loves a melon. My belly loves a pastry. My feet love dancing. See me, so often I've been at my front door just as soon as the day is dawning, ready to dance to the tambourine. The tambourine I could swear I heard playing, coming closer. Closer and closer. But then it's turned out to be just the wind. (*She laughs.*) You'll think me strange. I've had two husbands and fourteen sons. Six of them died. But I'm not sad. I'd like to live for ever. What I say is: look at the trees. How long they last. Look at a house of stone. How long it lasts. And then look at us, poor bloody women falling to bits for no reason at all.

YERMA. I'd like to ask you something.

OLD WOMAN. Would you? (*She looks at her.*) I know what you're going to say. These are things no one can talk about. (*She gets up.*)

YERMA (*stopping her*). Why not? Listening to you makes me trust you. For a long time now I've wanted to have a proper talk with an old woman like you. Because I want to find out. I really do. And you can tell me . . .

OLD WOMAN. What?

YERMA (*lowering her voice*). What you know. Why am I barren? Is there nothing else I can do with my life but look after budgies or put beautifully ironed curtains up in my window? No. You have to tell me what I need to do, because I will do whatever I have to. Even if you ask me to hit nails into the whites of my eyes.

OLD WOMAN. Me? I don't know nothing. I just opened my legs and started singing. Children come like the rain. Oooh . . . look at your body. Your beautiful body. Is there anyone so blind as to say otherwise? Step outside, and a stallion will neigh at the end of the street. Uy! Leave me alone, girl, don't make me speak. I am thinking things I do not wish to say out loud.

YERMA. Why not? With my husband, that's all I talk about.

OLD WOMAN. Listen. You like your husband?

YERMA. What do you mean?

OLD WOMAN. Do you like him? Do you want to be with him? Do you desire him?

YERMA. I don't know.

OLD WOMAN. When he comes to you does he make you shiver? When his mouth comes to yours do you go all dreamy? Tell me.

YERMA. No. I never felt like that. Never.

OLD WOMAN. Never? Not even when you were dancing?

YERMA (*trying to remember*). Maybe . . . once . . . with Victor . . .

OLD WOMAN. Go on.

YERMA. He put his arm round my waist and I couldn't say anything because I couldn't speak. And another time, Victor again, when I was fourteen and he was grown up, he picked me up to cross a stream and I was shaking so much my teeth started chattering. But the trouble was I felt ashamed.

OLD WOMAN. And your husband?

YERMA. With my husband it's something else again. My father gave me to him and I was happy. That's absolutely true. And the very first day I knew I was to be married to him I thought . . . I thought about children . . . And I looked at myself reflected in his eyes. Yes, and there I was, very small, at his bidding, as if I was my own child.

OLD WOMAN. Just the opposite to me. Perhaps that's why you haven't given birth. Listen, girl, when it comes to men you need to want them. They have to undo our hair and make us drink their mouths' saliva. That's what makes the world go round.

YERMA. Yours maybe, but not mine. I think things, many things, and I am sure the things I think my son will make come true. I gave myself to my husband for his sake, and I keep on giving myself just in case he comes. But never just to have pleasure.

OLD WOMAN. And that's why you're still empty!

YERMA. No. No, I'm not empty. I'm slowly filling with hate. Tell me, please, is it all my fault? Have I just got to keep looking for the man in the man? Is that all I can do? Or else, what are you supposed to think when he rolls over onto his side and goes to sleep, and you're just left there looking sadly up at the ceiling? Am I just supposed to keep on thinking of him, or of what could come out of my belly, shining? I don't know any more. Tell me. Please tell me. (*She kneels.*)

OLD WOMAN. Oh, you open flower! How lovely a creature you are! Let me be. Don't make me say more. I don't want to talk to you any more. These are things to do with honour, and I won't harm anyone's honour. You'll know what to do. But whatever you do, you should try to be less innocent.

YERMA (*sad*). Girls like me, girls who grow up in the country . . . all the doors are shut and bolted shut in our face. It's all words left only half-spoken, gestures only half-made, because these are all things that you're just not supposed to know . . . And you too, you keep quiet too, and then off you go looking like you know, like you know the answer to everything, but won't say it, won't tell me, even though you know I am dying of thirst.

OLD WOMAN. I would talk to a woman who was calmer. But not to you. I'm an old woman and I know what I'm saying.

YERMA. Then God help me.

OLD WOMAN. God's no use to you, dear. I've no time for him. When are you going to understand he doesn't exist? He's no use to you. Only men are.

YERMA. But why are you saying this? Why?

OLD WOMAN (*going*). Although there should be a god, even if only a tiny one, so he could send down his lightning to burn up the men whose seed is rotten and who poison the joy of the fields.

YERMA. I don't know what you're trying to tell me.

OLD WOMAN. Never mind. I know. Don't be sad. Keep hoping. You're still very young. What am I supposed to do for you?

She goes.

Two GIRLS *appear.*

GIRL 1. We just keep bumping into people everywhere!

YERMA. It's the olive harvest, so the men are out in the fields. It's just the old people left inside.

GIRL 2. You going back to the village?

YERMA. Yes, that's where I'm going.

GIRL 1. I'm in a real hurry. I left my baby asleep in the house alone.

YERMA. Then run. You can't leave a baby on his own. What if he got eaten by a sow?

GIRL 1. We don't keep pigs. But you're right. I'll run home.

YERMA. Yes. Run. These things happen. You've surely left him locked in.

GIRL 1. Obviously.

YERMA. I don't think you know how fragile a little child is. Something that seems completely harmless to us can finish him off. The slightest thing: a little needle, a sip of water.

GIRL 1. Yes, you're right. I'm running. The thing is I don't always think things through.

YERMA. Go!

GIRL 2. You wouldn't talk like that if you had four or five.

YERMA. Why not? I'm sure I would. Even if I had forty.

GIRL 2. Anyway, you and me, without children, we're much better off.

YERMA. Not me.

GIRL 2. I am. What a lot of work they are! But then my mum keeps on making me drink these disgusting herbs to help me get pregnant, and in October we've got to go to the shrine of the saint they say gives children to those who sincerely ask for them. My mum'll ask. I won't.

YERMA. Why did you get married?

GIRL 2. Because they made me. They make all of us. If things go on like this, everyone'll be married except girls of five! That's how it is. But then anyway you really get married long before you go to the church. It's the old women. They just can't leave these things alone. I'm nineteen years old and I hate cooking and washing. But that's what I've got to do all day. Things I hate doing. And why? Why does my husband need to be my husband? We do exactly the same things we used to do before we got married. It's just old people's silliness.

YERMA. Shush. Don't say such things.

GIRL 2. You're going to say I'm mad too. 'Mad. She's mad!' (*Laughs.*) I'll tell you the only thing I've learned from life: that the whole world is stuck in their houses doing things they hate doing. People are so much better off out in the street. I go to the stream. I climb the tower to ring the bells, I can have a wee drink of anís.

YERMA. You're just a girl.

GIRL 2. Yes. Obviously, but I'm not mad. (*Laughs.*)

YERMA. Is it your mother who lives right up at the top of the village?

GIRL 2. Yes.

YERMA. In the very last house?

GIRL 2. Yes.

YERMA. What's her name?

GIRL 2. Dolores. Why do you want to know?

YERMA. I don't know. I was just . . .

GIRL 2. Look at you . . . Anyway, I'm off to give my husband his food. (*Laughs.*) It just goes to show. What a shame I can't just call him my man! Right? 'There she goes. Mad she is. Mad!' (*She goes off laughing cheerfully.*) Byee!

VICTOR'S VOICE (*singing*).
Shepherd, why sleep alone?
Shepherd, why sleep alone?
You'd sleep so much better
On my mattress at home.
Shepherd, why sleep alone?

YERMA (*listening*).
Shepherd, why sleep alone?
Shepherd, why sleep alone?
You'd sleep so much better
On my mattress at home.
Your shirt is stiff with frost,
Shepherd, and your mattress of grey stone.
Winter's splintered straw for a blanket
For your pillow, just thistles and thorns.
You spend the winter's night alone.
If you hear a woman sighing
See a woman in your dreams
It's just the wind blowing
The water eddying in the streams.

About to leave, she bumps into VICTOR *as he enters.*

VICTOR. Where's she going, this beauty?

YERMA. Was it you who was singing?

VICTOR. It was me.

YERMA. You sing so well! It's the first time I've heard you.

VICTOR. Is it?

YERMA. Such a strong voice. It's like a mountain stream. It just flows out your mouth so naturally.

VICTOR. I'm happy.

YERMA. It's true.

VICTOR. And you are sad.

YERMA. No, I'm not sad. But I do have reason to be.

VICTOR. A husband who's even sadder than you are.

YERMA. Him, yes. He's a dried-up kind of person.

VICTOR. He's always been like that. (*Pause.* YERMA *has sat down.*) Did you come to bring him his meal?

YERMA. Yes. (*She looks at him. Pause.*) What happened there? (*She points to his face.*)

VICTOR. Where?

YERMA (*getting up and going to* VICTOR). Here . . . on your cheek. It looks like a burn.

VICTOR. It's nothing.

YERMA. I just wondered.

Pause.

VICTOR. Maybe I caught the sun . . .

YERMA. Maybe . . .

Pause. The silence deepens and without the slightest outward sign an intense struggle begins between the two of them.

(*Trembling*) Do you hear?

VICTOR. Hear what?

YERMA. There's a baby crying.

VICTOR (*listening*). I can't hear it.

YERMA. I could have sworn I heard a baby cry.

VICTOR. Did you?

YERMA. Very close. As if it was drowning.

VICTOR. There's always a lot of kids round here. They come to rob the fruit trees.

YERMA. It wasn't them. It was a baby.

Pause.

VICTOR. I can't hear anything.

YERMA. I must be hearing things.

She stares at him, and VICTOR *looks at her, and then slowly looks away, as if afraid.*

Enter JUAN.

JUAN. What are you doing here?

YERMA. Talking.

VICTOR. Good day. (*He goes.*)

JUAN. You should be at home.

YERMA. It was nice here.

JUAN. I can't imagine what was so nice.

YERMA. I was listening to the birds singing.

JUAN. People are going to start to talk.

YERMA (*fiercely*). Juan, what are you implying?

JUAN. I'm not talking about you. I'm talking about what people might say.

YERMA. I hope they all choke!

JUAN. Don't use such expressions. A woman shouldn't speak like that. They make you ugly.

YERMA. I wish I was a woman!

JUAN. We won't talk about it further. Go back home.

Pause.

YERMA. As you wish. When shall I expect you?

JUAN. I won't come home tonight. I've to be out here to water the crops. There's not much water, and tonight it's my turn to get it. I need to stay here till dawn to make sure no one steals it. I'll be here till dawn. Go to bed and sleep.

YERMA (*with deep feeling*). I'll sleep! (*She goes.*)

Curtain.

ACT TWO

Scene One

A rushing stream in which the village women do their washing. The
WASHERWOMEN *are on various levels. They sing with the curtain*
still closed.

WASHERWOMEN.
  Cold is the water
  Washing this hour
  Warm is your laughter
  Like jasmine flower.

WASHERWOMAN 1. I don't like to gossip . . .

WASHERWOMAN 3. But everyone's doing it.

WASHERWOMAN 4. And there's no harm in it.

WASHERWOMAN 5. No smoke without fire.

WASHERWOMAN 4. No fire without smoke.

  They laugh.

WASHERWOMAN 5. So people say.

WASHERWOMAN 1. But no one really knows.

WASHERWOMAN 4. One thing for sure is that the husband
  has brought in his two sisters to live with them.

WASHERWOMAN 5. The old maids?

WASHERWOMAN 4. Them. The ones who look after the
  church and now have to look after his wife. I wouldn't want
  them in my house.

WASHERWOMAN 1. Why not?

WASHERWOMAN 4. They're so creepy. They're like those
  slimy plants with the big green leaves that you see growing
  on a freshly dug grave. They're greasy with candle wax. I
  think they must cook with the oil from the lamps in church.

WASHERWOMAN 3. And they're in her house already?

WASHERWOMAN 4. Since yesterday. And the husband's out working on his land.

WASHERWOMAN 1. Can someone tell me what's supposed to have happened?

WASHERWOMAN 5. Remember how cold it was the night before last? Well, she spent the whole night out in it. Sitting on her own doorstep. She spent the night before last sitting out on the doorstep in spite of the cold.

WASHERWOMAN 1. But why?

WASHERWOMAN 4. Because she can't stand being inside her own house.

WASHERWOMAN 5. She's just a withered old bitch that'll never have kids. They're all the same. She should stay out of sight and mind her own business. But instead they go walking naked on their rooftops or sit out all night on their doorsteps.

WASHERWOMAN 1. What right have you to say things like that? It's not her fault she doesn't have children.

WASHERWOMAN 4. People have children who really want them. There's just some that are too weak, too delicate, too soft and too posh to be able to bear having a stretch mark.

They laugh.

WASHERWOMAN 3. So they put on red lipstick and black eye-shadow and their best low-cut dress and go off looking for another man who is not their husband.

WASHERWOMAN 5. And that's the way it is.

WASHERWOMAN 1. But have any of you actually seen her with another man?

WASHERWOMAN 4. Well, we haven't. But people have.

WASHERWOMAN 1. Strange how it's always someone else!

WASHERWOMAN 5. It's twice she's been seen with a man. That's what they say.

WASHERWOMAN 2. And what were they doing?

WASHERWOMAN 4. Talking.

WASHERWOMAN 1. Talking is not a crime.

WASHERWOMAN 5. But they were also looking. And looking is something else. My mother used to tell me. A woman looking at a bunch of flowers is one thing. A woman looking at a man's thighs is quite another. And she looks at him.

WASHERWOMAN 1. But who?

WASHERWOMAN 4. Someone. Don't you know? Think about it. Do you want me to spell it out? (*Laughter.*) And even when she's not looking at him, because she's on her own, and he's not in front of her, he's still pictured in her eyes.

WASHERWOMAN 1. You're a liar!

A moment of fierce conflict.

WASHERWOMAN 5. What about the husband?

WASHERWOMAN 3. It's like he was deaf and blind. Paralysed. Like a lizard in the noonday sun.

They laugh.

WASHERWOMAN 1. If only they had children. All this would sort itself out.

WASHERWOMAN 2. All this would sort itself out if some people knew their place.

WASHERWOMAN 4. It gets worse and worse in that house. Hour by hour. It's like being in hell. Her and her two sisters-in-law never say a word to each other. They spend all day whitewashing the walls, polishing the coppers, cleaning all the glasses and waxing the floors. And the more the house gleams on the outside, the muckier it is on the inside.

WASHERWOMAN 1. It's his fault. It's his. When a husband can't father a child he needs to take care of his wife.

WASHERWOMAN 4. No. It's her fault. She's got a tongue like a razor.

WASHERWOMAN 1. What's got into you to make you say such horrible things?

WASHERWOMAN 4. And what's got into you to make you think you can tell me what to do?

WASHERWOMAN 5. Quiet!

Laughter.

WASHERWOMAN 1. If I had a darning needle I'd sew up the mouths of malicious tongues.

WASHERWOMAN 5. Shut up!

WASHERWOMAN 4. And I'd cover the breasts of hypocrites.

WASHERWOMAN 5. Be quiet! Can't you see who's coming? It's the aunts!

Mutterings. YERMA's *two* SISTERS-IN-LAW *enter. They are dressed in mourning. They begin to wash in the midst of the silence. We hear goat bells.*

WASHERWOMAN 1. Have the shepherds gone?

WASHERWOMAN 3. Yes. The flocks are all leaving now.

WASHERWOMAN 4 (*breathing in*). I love the smell of sheep.

WASHERWOMAN 3. Do you?

WASHERWOMAN 4. And why not? It smells of such familiar things. Just as I like the smell of the red mud brought down by the river in winter.

WASHERWOMAN 3. You're crazy.

WASHERWOMAN 5 (*looking out*). They've joined all the flocks together.

WASHERWOMAN 4. As if to flood everywhere with wool. They trample over everything. If the young wheat had eyes, it would tremble to see them coming.

WASHERWOMAN 3. And how they run! What a crowd!

WASHERWOMAN 1. Out they all go. None are left behind.

WASHERWOMAN 4. Wait . . . I'm not sure . . . Yes. there's one flock missing.

WASHERWOMAN 5. Whose?

WASHERWOMAN 4. Victor's.

The two SISTERS-IN-LAW *raise their heads to see.*

Cold is the water
Washing this hour
Warm is your laughter
Like jasmine flower.

I'm dreaming of living
In the tiny white snowfall
Of the jasmine's white flower.

WASHERWOMAN 1.
Pity the woman whose breasts are dry
Barren as the desert
Under the empty sky

WASHERWOMAN 5.
Tell me does your husband
Keep seed in your house
So the water starts singing
In your linen blouse

WASHERWOMAN 6.
Your blouse floats like a ship
By the bend of the river
Its sails fill with wind

WASHERWOMAN 3.
The clothes of my baby
I've come here to wash
They're teaching the water
To be clear as glass

WASHERWOMAN 2.
My husband is coming
Down the high road to eat
A rose he will bring me
And I'll give him three

WASHERWOMAN 5.
My husband is coming
Down the low road to dine
His hands full of fire
Like hot coals are mine

WASHERWOMAN 4.
    My husband is coming
    Through the air to his bed
    I give him red poppies
    His roses are red

WASHERWOMAN 3.
    Flower lies with flower
    The summer heat warms the seed

WASHERWOMAN 4.
    When winter sets the whole world shivering and shaking
    Still the belly lies open to the birds that are waking

WASHERWOMAN 1.
    Time to be moaning in between the sheets

WASHERWOMAN 4.
    Time to be singing in the bed off the streets

WASHERWOMAN 5.
    When the man brings in bread and brings in the crown

WASHERWOMAN 4.
    When arms are embracing what's up and what's down

WASHERWOMAN 5.
    Because our throat is open to the golden light

WASHERWOMAN 4.
    The branches are bending, the flowers are bright

WASHERWOMAN 5.
    The mountains are covered by the wings of the wind.

WASHERWOMAN 6 (*appearing high up at the top of the torrent*).
    So a baby can melt
    The cold fingers of dawn

WASHERWOMAN 4.
    So the coral's branches of red
    Can crown our fierce heads

WASHERWOMAN 5.
    And the sailors sing gladness
    On the waves of the sea

WASHERWOMAN 1.
    A child, a little one

WASHERWOMAN 2.
And the doves spread their wings

WASHERWOMAN 3.
A child laughing, a loved one

WASHERWOMAN 4.
And the men moving forward
Like bold rutting stags

WASHERWOMAN 5.
Oh, the joy the joy the joy
Of the round fertile belly!

WASHERWOMAN 2.
Oh, the joy the joy the joy
Of the navel, the tender cup of marvels!

WASHERWOMAN 1.
Pity the woman whose breasts are dry
Barren as the desert
Under the empty sky

WASHERWOMAN 4.
Let the child shine!

WASHERWOMAN 5.
Let him run!

WASHERWOMAN 4.
Let him shine again!

WASHERWOMAN 3.
Let him sing!

WASHERWOMAN 2.
Let him hide!

WASHERWOMAN 3.
Let him sing again.

WASHERWOMAN 6.
Of the dawn that my baby
Carries in his eyes!

WASHERWOMAN 4 (*and they all sing with her in chorus*).
Cold is the water
Washing this hour

Warm is your laughter
Like jasmine flower.

They all laugh together and beat the clothes together to wash them on the stones.

Curtain.

Scene Two

YERMA*'s house. Nightfall.* JUAN *is sitting. His two* SISTERS *stand.*

JUAN. You're saying she just went out?

SISTER 1 *nods in reply.*

She must be getting water from the well. But you know I don't like her to go out alone. (*Pause.*) You can lay the table.

SISTER 2 *goes out.*

I've worked hard for the food on my table. (*To* SISTER 1.) Yesterday was a hard day. I was pruning the apple trees. At the end of the day I started to wonder why I work so hard when I can't pick an apple and eat it myself. I've had enough. (*He passes his hands over his face. Pause.*) Still not back . . . One of you should go out with her, because that's why you're here. That's why you're eating at my table and drinking my wine. My life is out in the fields but my honour and self-respect are here. And my honour is also your honour.

SISTER 1 *nods her head.*

Don't take it to heart.

YERMA *comes in with two large water jugs. She stops on the threshold.*

Have you come from the spring?

YERMA. So we could have some cool water with our meal.

Enter SISTER 2.

How is the land?

JUAN. Yesterday I was pruning the apple trees.

YERMA *puts down the water jugs. Pause.*

YERMA. Are you staying in?

JUAN. I have to take care of the flock. You know that's the owner's responsibility.

YERMA. I know that only too well. There's no need to say it again.

JUAN. Each man must live his life.

YERMA. And each woman must live hers. I'm not asking you to stay at home. I have all I need here. Your sisters feed me very well. Roast lamb, soft white bread and the finest cheese on the menu for your wife, and good green grass on the hillside for your sheep. You can set your mind at rest.

JUAN. Having your mind at rest means living in peace.

YERMA. And don't you?

JUAN. No.

YERMA. There's no point talking about it.

JUAN. But don't you know how I want life to be? Sheep in the sheepfold. Women in the home. You go out too much. Haven't I said that again and again?

YERMA. Yes. So you have. Women in the home. When their homes are not like a grave. When beds get broken and sheets get worn out with use. But not here. Every night when I go to bed, my bed is as new and as unused as if we had just bought it in a shop in the city.

JUAN. You know very well I'm right to complain. That I'm right to stay on my guard!

YERMA. On your guard against what? I don't do you any harm. I live under your thumb, and what I suffer I keep to myself. Nailed to my flesh. Every day that passes will be worse. And we'll never talk about it. I'll do what I can to bear what I have to bear, but don't ask me for any more. If all of a sudden I could turn into an old woman with a withered mouth, I might be able to smile and live with you. But just now, just leave me alone. Leave me with what's nailed into me.

JUAN. You are talking in a way I cannot understand. I don't deprive you of anything. I'm always asking the neighbours for things I know you like to have. I'm not perfect, I know that, but I want to live with you peacefully and quietly. Without fuss. I want to sleep in the open and know that you are sleeping too.

YERMA. I don't sleep. I can't sleep.

JUAN. Is there anything you need? Tell me. (*Pause.*) Answer!

YERMA (*with a clear intention and looking fixedly at her husband*). Yes. Yes, there is something.

Pause.

JUAN. It's always that. After more than five years. I'd almost forgotten all about it.

YERMA. But you are not me. The men have another life: with their sheep and their crops. The things they talk about. But with us women there's just children. And how to look after them. That's all there is.

JUAN. Not everyone's the same. Why don't you look after one of your brother's children? I wouldn't mind.

YERMA. I don't want to look after other people's children. I can feel my arms freezing when I hold them.

JUAN. And that's exactly the attitude that's distressing you. So you end up not behaving as you ought. And instead you keep banging your head against a stone wall.

YERMA. A stone wall which shouldn't be a wall. The fact it's there is a kind of crime. When what it should be is a basket of flowers and a jug of sweet water.

JUAN. All I ever get from you is anguish and anxiety and grief. But at the end of the day you have just got to get used to things.

YERMA. I came here not to get used to things. When they tie a scarf round my head to stop my mouth dropping open. When they have to jam my hands together inside my coffin. That's when I'll have got used to things.

JUAN. So what do you want?

YERMA. I want to drink water, and there is no water to drink and no glass to drink it in. I want to climb to the summit of the mountain, and I have no feet to walk with. I want to embroider my dress, and I have neither needle nor thread.

JUAN. You're just not a proper woman and you'll ruin any man who can't stand up to you.

YERMA. I don't know who I am. Let me be. Let me try to unburden myself. I have failed you in nothing.

JUAN. I don't want people to point the finger at me. That is why I want this door to be kept shut and for everyone to stay in their home.

SISTER 1 *slowly comes onto the stage and goes up to a glass-fronted cupboard.*

YERMA. Talking to people is not a crime.

JUAN. But it can look like one.

SISTER 2 *enters, goes to the water container, and fills up a jug.*

(*Lowering his voice.*) I haven't the strength for this. When they talk to you, keep your mouth shut. Remember you're a married woman.

YERMA (*astounded*). Me? Married?

JUAN. And remember: families need honour and they need self-respect, and these things are everyone's responsibility.

SISTER 2 *slowly leaves with the water jug.*

But in the very veins of our body our honour flows sluggish and weak.

SISTER 1 *leaves with a serving dish, in a way that almost recalls a church procession. Pause.*

Forgive me.

YERMA *looks at her husband. He raises his head to look at her. His gaze falters.*

Although you look at me in a way that means I should not say 'Forgive me'. I should impose myself instead, and lock you away. Because that's what being a husband means.

The two SISTERS appear in the doorway.

YERMA. Please don't talk about it any more. Let's leave these things be.

Pause.

JUAN. Let's go in to eat.

The two SISTERS *go inside. Pause.*

Did you hear me?

YERMA (*gently*). You eat with your sisters. I don't feel hungry just now.

JUAN. Whatever you say. (*He goes in.*)

YERMA (*dreamily*).
Oh, the road I travel is paved with thorn
The door of love is shut against me
I'm asking to suffer the birth pangs of a baby
And all I'm given are limp flowers
Wilting under a half-formed moon!
These should be two springs of warm milk
But instead in my thickened coarsened flesh
They feel like the hoof beats of a wounded animal.
My breasts have been blinded.
They're doves without eyes or whiteness.
My blood is a prisoner going round and round my body
And my pulse nails thorns to my throat.
You have to come, my child, my loved one,
You have to come, like the ocean gives salt,
Trees give their fruit, and our wombs
Keep tender children safe in warm darkness
Like the cloud that carries sweet rain.

She looks towards the door.

Maria! Why are you rushing so fast by my door?

Enter MARIA.

MARIA. I'm carrying my baby and I can't bear to see you cry.

YERMA. I understand. (*She takes the baby and sits down.*)

MARIA. I'm so sorry I make you so envious.

YERMA. I'm not envious. I'm just poor.

MARIA. Don't cry.

YERMA. What else can I do when I see you and all the other women so full of flowers and me so useless in the midst of so much beauty!

MARIA. But you've other things in your life. If you'd just listen to me, you could be happy.

YERMA. The country woman who has no children is as useless as a handful of thistles. And worse. There's a kind of badness to her. And I'm saying that even though I belong to this godforsaken wasteland.

MARIA *makes a move to take back her baby*.

Yes. Take him. He'll be happier with you. I don't seem to have a mother's hands.

MARIA. Why are you telling me this?

YERMA (*getting up*). Because I'm weary, so weary of having arms that are made to hold someone and that I'm never able to use as they should. Because I just can't bear it. It insults me, it humiliates and it degrades me to see how the wheat comes to harvest and the springs keep giving water and the sheep keep giving birth to lambs and even the dogs. And it's like the whole of the countryside is going out of its way to show me its adorable sleepy warm babies, while instead of the feeding mouth of my child here, and here, all I feel is like the dull thud of a heavy hammer.

MARIA. I don't like what you're saying.

YERMA. You women who have children can't imagine what it's like to be us who don't. You're just so innocent of everything, and you don't know, you don't know. Just as someone swimming in sweet water has no idea what it feels like to be thirsty.

MARIA. I don't want to repeat what I always say to you.

YERMA. Every day I want more and I hope less.

MARIA. That's not good.

YERMA. I'm going to end up thinking I'm my own son. Night after night I go down to feed the oxen, which is something I never used to do, because it's not woman's work, but I do it now, and when I walk on the shed's flagstones my footsteps sound to me like the footsteps of a man.

MARIA. All God's creatures have their reasons to be.

YERMA. In spite of everything, don't hate me. You see how I am.

MARIA. What about his sisters?

YERMA. Kill me and leave me to rot unburied if you ever see me speak a word to them.

MARIA. What about your husband?

YERMA. It's three against one.

MARIA. What are they thinking?

YERMA. They imagine things. As people do when they've got a bad conscience. They think there has to be another man I'm after, and what they don't understand is that even if there was someone in my family our honour always comes first. They stand in my way like boulders . . . But what they don't understand is that, if I want, I can be water of a mountain torrent that will wash them away.

One SISTER *comes in and goes out carrying a loaf of bread.*

MARIA. Whatever happens, I'm sure your husband still loves you.

YERMA. My husband puts bread on the table and a roof over my head.

MARIA. Dear God, the things you're going through and all you have to bear. Try to remember what Jesus went through as he was hanging on the cross!

They are standing by the door.

YERMA (*looking at the baby*). He's woken up.

MARIA. Soon he'll start to sing.

YERMA. He's got your eyes. Did you know that? Have you seen? (*Crying.*) He's got your eyes!

YERMA *gently pushes* MARIA *out of the door, and she silently goes.* YERMA *is about to go to the door her husband went through.*

GIRL 2. Pssst!

YERMA (*turning back*). What is it?

GIRL 2. I was waiting for her to leave. My mother's waiting for you.

YERMA. Is she on her own?

GIRL 2. She's with two neighbours.

YERMA. Tell her to wait a minute.

GIRL 2. But are you coming? You're not afraid?

YERMA. I'm coming.

GIRL 2. Rather you than me!

YERMA. Tell them to wait, even if I come late!

VICTOR *enters.*

VICTOR. Is Juan in?

YERMA. Yes.

GIRL 2 (*conspiratorially*). I'll bring you the blouse then.

YERMA. When you can.

The GIRL *leaves.*

Sit down.

VICTOR. I'm best to stand.

YERMA (*calls out for her husband*). Juan!

VICTOR. I've come to say goodbye.

YERMA (*shivers a little, but returns to her state of apparent calm*). Are you going with your brothers?

VICTOR. That's what my father wants.

YERMA. He must be getting old.

VICTOR. Yes. He's getting on.

Pause.

YERMA. It's a good idea for you to move.

VICTOR. Everywhere's the same.

YERMA. No. I'd get right out of here.

VICTOR. It's all the same. The sheep are the same. They all have wool.

YERMA. That may be true for men, but for us women it's another story. I never heard a man eat an apple and say: 'These apples taste so good!' You just take what's yours without noticing the joy in it. All I can say about me and this place is that I have learnt to hate the water that comes from its wells.

VICTOR. Maybe.

The stage is now in a gentle twilight. Pause.

YERMA. Victor.

VICTOR. What?

YERMA. Why are you going? People like you here.

VICTOR. I behaved as I should.

YERMA. Oh yes. You were very correct. When you were still a boy you carried me once in your arms. Do you remember? We never know how things may turn out.

VICTOR. Everything changes.

YERMA. Some things don't change. Some things get bricked in behind walls and they can't change because no one can hear them.

VICTOR. That's true.

SISTER 2 *appears and slowly goes to the door where she stands lit by the light of the setting sun.*

YERMA. Because if they could suddenly get out and scream, they would scream so loud the sound would fill the world.

VICTOR. That wouldn't help. Water flows down its channel, sheep belong to the sheepfold, and the man belongs to the plough.

YERMA. What a shame I can't appreciate the wisdom of the old!

We hear the long melancholic sounds of the shepherd's conch shells.

VICTOR. They're bringing the flocks home.

JUAN (*entering*). Are you away now?

VICTOR. I want to reach the port before daybreak.

JUAN. Have you any complaint?

VICTOR. No. Not against you. You always paid on time.

JUAN (*to* YERMA). I bought his sheep.

YERMA. Really?

VICTOR (*to* YERMA). They're all yours.

YERMA. I didn't know that.

JUAN (*complacently*). That's what's happened.

VICTOR. Your husband will be so rich.

YERMA. Money comes to the hands of the man who works for it.

The SISTER *who was at the doorway goes inside.*

JUAN. We'll have nowhere to put so many sheep.

YERMA (*sombrely*). The earth is wide.

Pause.

JUAN. I'll walk you to the stream.

VICTOR. I wish this house all happiness.

He shakes YERMA *by the hand.*

YERMA. God hear you. Goodbye.

VICTOR *takes his leave, and then, in response to an imperceptible signal from* YERMA, *turns back.*

VICTOR. Did you say something?

YERMA (*charged with emotion*). I said goodbye.

VICTOR. Goodbye.

They go. YERMA *casts an anguished look at her hand, which has just touched* VICTOR's. *She heads rapidly to the left and takes a cloak.*

GIRL 2 (*quietly, putting up her hood*). Let's go.

YERMA. Let's go.

They go out cautiously. The stage is now almost dark. SISTER 1 *enters with a candle that gives no more than its natural light. She goes to the back of the stage looking for* YERMA. *We hear the conch shells calling the sheep.*

SISTER 1 (*in a low voice*). Yerma!

Enter SISTER 2. *They give each other a look and head for the door.*

SISTER 2 (*louder*). Yerma! (*She goes out.*)

SISTER 1 (*also going to the door, and calling out harshly*). Yerma!

She goes out. We hear the conch shells and the horn of the shepherds calling their sheep. The stage is in almost total darkness.

Curtain.

ACT THREE

Scene One

The house belonging to DOLORES, *the wise woman and witch. Dawn is breaking.*

Enter YERMA *with* DOLORES *and two* OLD WOMEN.

DOLORES. You've been brave.

OLD WOMAN 1. Nothing as strong as the heart's desire.

OLD WOMAN 2. But it was too dark in the graveyard.

DOLORES. There's been so many times I've spoken these prayers in the graveyard with women who wanted children and they've all been afraid. Every single one but you.

YERMA. I came to get a child. And I trust you.

DOLORES. You're right to. If I have ever lied may my tongue be covered in ants like a corpse's. The last time I did that prayer it was for a beggarwoman, who was barren for longer than you, and her belly softened in so beautiful a way that she had twins down there by the river because they didn't give her time to get to a house, and she herself brought them to me wrapped up in a headscarf so I could sort them.

YERMA. And she could walk all the way from the river?

DOLORES. That's what she did. Her shoes and her petticoats were soaked in blood. But her face was shining.

YERMA. And there was nothing wrong with her?

DOLORES. What could go wrong? God is God.

YERMA. Of course. Nothing could happen. She just had to take hold of the wee things and wash them in living water. Animals lick their young, don't they? The idea doesn't disgust me at all. I think that new mothers must be lit up by a light inside them and that the babies sleep for hours and hours and hours just listening to this stream of warm milk that fills their breasts so the babies can suck and suck and take their pleasure until they don't need any more, till their heads drop back, have another wee drop my baby, and their faces and their chests are spattered with the white drops.

DOLORES. I assure you. You will have a son.

YERMA. I will have him because I have to. Or the world makes no sense. At times when I think that he will never never come it's like a wave of fire that comes up from my feet and burns everything up, so that the men who walk down the street and the bulls and the stones just look like bits of cotton wool. And I ask myself, what are they doing here?

OLD WOMAN 1. It's right and proper for a married woman to want a son, but if she doesn't have one, why go through all this agony? The most important thing is just to let life happen. I'm not criticising. You saw how I helped you do the prayers. But what do you expect to give your child? Can you give him a meadow? Can you give him happiness? Can you give him a throne of gold?

YERMA. I don't think about tomorrow. I think about today. You're an old old woman and life's like a book you finished reading years ago. I feel I have no freedom. I have thirst. I want to hold my son in my arms, that's the only way I can have peace. Listen to this, and don't get too upset by what I'm saying: even if I knew my son was really going to make me suffer and beat me even and drag me through the streets by the hair, his birth would still fill me with joy. Because it's better to be made to cry by a living man who beats us than be crying for a ghost that's been sitting on my heart for year after year.

OLD WOMAN 1. You're too young to listen to advice. But still, while you're waiting for the grace and mercy of God, you'd do better to take refuge in your husband's love.

YERMA. Oh God! You've just put your finger on my body's deepest wound.

DOLORES. You've got a good husband.

YERMA (*getting up*). Oh yes, he's good. He's very good. So what? I wish he were bad. No. He counts his sheep by day

and he counts his money by night. And when he covers me,
when he tries to inseminate me, he's just doing it out of
duty and he's as cold as a corpse. And me, me who's always
been disgusted by women on heat, and that moment . . .
that moment I wish I were a mountain of fire.

DOLORES. Yerma!

YERMA. There's nothing indecent about me. Nothing
unchaste. But I know where children come from. They
come from a woman and a man. Oh, if only, if only I could
have them alone!

DOLORES. Think about your husband. He must be
suffering too.

YERMA. He doesn't suffer. The thing about him is he doesn't
want a child.

OLD WOMAN 1. Don't say that!

YERMA. I can tell it from the way he looks at me. And
because he doesn't want one, he can't give me one. He
doesn't want one, he doesn't want one, yet he's the only way
I can get one. Because of my honour and my family. He's
the only way.

OLD WOMAN 1 (*afraid*). It'll soon be dawn. You should go
home.

DOLORES. They'll be taking the flocks out very soon and
you shouldn't be seen alone.

YERMA. I needed to get that off my chest. How often do I
say the prayers?

DOLORES. The laurel prayer you say twice, and then at
midday you say the prayer of Saint Anne. And then when
you're pregnant you bring me the bushel of wheat you
promised.

OLD WOMAN 1. The light is breaking over the mountain. Go.

DOLORES. They'll be opening their front doors now. You'll
have to take the back path.

YERMA (*discouraged*). I don't know why I came!

DOLORES. Are you sorry you did?

YERMA. No.

DOLORES (*disturbed*). If you're afraid, I'll walk you down to the corner.

OLD WOMAN 1 (*anxious*). It'll be broad daylight before you get to your door.

We hear voices.

DOLORES. Listen! (*They listen.*)

OLD WOMAN 1. It's no one. Go with God.

YERMA *goes to the door and that moment someone knocks on it. The three women stand stock-still.*

DOLORES. Who is it?

VOICE. It's me.

YERMA. Open the door.

DOLORES *hesitates.*

I said open the door!

We hear mutterings. JUAN *and the two* SISTERS *appear.*

SISTER 2. There she is!

YERMA. Here I am!

JUAN. What are you doing in this place? If I could I'd shout out loud enough to wake the whole village so they could see where my house's honour has gone. But I have to stifle everything because you are my wife.

YERMA. If I could shout, I'd be shouting out too, so that even the dead could get up from their graves and see me clothed in all innocence.

JUAN. No! I can put up with everything but that! You are deceiving me, you weave around me your web of deceit and lies. And I'm a simple man, a straightforward man who works the earth, and I can't deal with your deviousness.

DOLORES. Juan!

JUAN. And not a word from you!

DOLORES (*fiercely*). Your wife has done nothing wrong.

JUAN. She's been undermining me since the day we got married. She's got two needles for eyes and she sticks them into me. She never sleeps at night. She stays awake all the time staring at me and infecting my bedroom with her misery.

YERMA. Shut up!

JUAN. I can't stand it any more. You'd have to be made out of stone to put up with a woman who wants to stick her fingers right into your heart and who goes out into the street at night looking for what? Tell me! Looking for what? The streets are full of men. And you don't go out the door to pick flowers.

YERMA. I won't let you say one word more. You imagine that you and your people are the only ones who are honourable, and you ignore the fact that my family has never had to hide anything from anybody. Come here. Come up to me and smell my clothes, come here and do it! And see if you notice any smell that is not yours, that does not belong to your body. You're stripping me naked in the middle of the village square and spitting on me. I know I'm your wife and you have the right to do whatever you want, but don't you dare impute a man's name on my breasts.

JUAN. It's not something I do. It's something you do with your behaviour, and the people are beginning say so openly. When I come up to a group of people, they all fall silent; when I go to weigh the flour, they all fall silent; and even at night in the fields, when I wake up, it seems to me the branches of the trees are falling silent too.

YERMA. I know there's a bad wind blowing and it's stirring up the wheat on the threshing floor. And is the wheat good? Or is it rotten? You should look and see.

JUAN. What I want to know is why a woman should be out looking for something at all hours of the night.

YERMA (*embracing her husband with a sudden impulse*). I'm looking for you. I am looking for you. It's you I'm looking for day and night without finding any shade in which to breathe. It's your blood and your protection I desire.

JUAN. Get away from me.

YERMA. Don't drive me away. Find a way to love me.

JUAN. Leave me alone!

YERMA. Look at me. I am abandoned and alone. As if the moon had to look for herself in the sky. Look at me! (*She looks at him.*)

JUAN (*looks at her then abruptly withdraws his gaze*). Just leave me alone!

DOLORES. Juan!

YERMA *falls to the ground.*

YERMA (*loudly*). When I went out to look for flowers I came slap up against a stone wall. Ay! Ay! And over and over again I keep banging my head against it! And I can't stop!

JUAN. Be quiet. Let's go home.

DOLORES. Oh my god!

YERMA (*shouting*). I curse the mother who gave me this wish to have children! I curse my desire so deep in my blood I keep searching for my children and can never find them!

JUAN. I said be quiet!

DOLORES. There are people coming! Keep your voices down!

YERMA. I don't care if people come. Let my voice at least be free, now I am entering the darkest point of this well. (*She gets up.*) Let this beautiful thing at least leave my body and fill the air.

We hear voices.

DOLORES. They're going to walk past here.

JUAN. Silence.

YERMA. It's that. It's that. Silence. Don't you worry.

JUAN. Home. Now!

YERMA. That's it! That's it! And it's no use wringing my hands! It's one thing to wish with the head . . .

JUAN. Be quiet!

YERMA (*in a low voice*). It's one thing to wish with the head
but whether the body actually responds is something else
altogether. This accursed body. What is written is written,
and I'm not going to fight against the waves of the sea. I
can't. May my mouth stay soundless and dumb! (*She leaves.*)

Curtain.

Final Scene

*Outside a hermitage on the high mountain. Downstage, some cartwheels
and blankets form a rough shelter, where* YERMA *sits. The* WOMEN
come in with offerings. They are barefoot. Also on stage is the cheerful
PAGAN OLD WOMAN *of the first act.*

A song behind the closed curtain:

When you were single, my lovely
We never could meet.
But now that you're married, my lovely
Your body I'll greet.
When the clocks strike twelve, my lovely,
I will strip you bare.
Join the pilgrims, my lovely,
And I'll meet you there.

OLD WOMAN (*sarcastically*). You sure you've drunk the holy
water?

WOMAN 1. Yes.

OLD WOMAN. And next you've got to see the saint.

WOMAN 2. We believe in his power.

OLD WOMAN. So you come here to ask the saint for
children. And all that happens is that 3every year more and
more single men come too. It's a miracle. (*She laughs.*)

WOMAN 1. If you don't believe in it, why do you come?

OLD WOMAN. To watch. I love to watch. And take care of
my son. Last year two men knifed each other over some
barren wife and I want to be on guard. And in the end I
come because I want to.

WOMAN 1. God forgive you! (*They go in.*)

OLD WOMAN (*sarcastically*). And God forgive you and all.

She goes. Enter MARIA *with* GIRL 1.

GIRL 1. And did she come?

MARIA. Their cart's over there. I had to work hard to get them to come. She's spent the whole of the last month just sitting. Just sitting in her chair. I'm frightened of her. She's got an idea in her head. I don't know what it is. But it's obvious it's something wicked.

GIRL 1. I came with my sister. She's been coming for eight years. And nothing.

MARIA. The one who's meant to have children will have them.

GIRL 1. That's what I say.

We hear voices.

MARIA. I never liked this festival. Let's go to the threshing floors, where the people are.

GIRL 1. Last year when it got dark, some boys got hold of my sister's breasts.

MARIA. For miles all around all you hear are dirty words.

GIRL 1. I saw forty barrels of wine just round the back of the church . . . Forty! I counted them.

MARIA. There's crowds and crowds of men coming from all around.

We hear voices. YERMA *comes in with* WOMEN *going to the church. Their feet are bare and they carry fluted candles. Night begins to fall.*

YERMA.
Lord, may the rose come in flower
And may I not be left in darkness.

WOMAN 2.
Lord, may the yellow rose flower
On her fading yellow flesh.

YERMA.
Lord, in the belly of your servant
Light the earth's dark flame.

CHORUS OF WOMEN.
> Lord, may the rose come in flower
> And may I not be left in darkness.

They kneel.

YERMA.
> Heaven has gardens
> Where roses grow in joy
> Among all the flowers
> The miraculous rose.
> Like a guardian archangel
> Or a ray of light from the dawn.
> Its eyes are like agonies
> Its wings are like storms.
> Its sap of warm milk
> Gives life to its leaves.
> Its warm drops are falling
> To moisten the faces
> Of the tranquil stars.
> O Lord, may the yellow rose flower
> On my fading flesh.

They get up.

WOMAN 2.
> Lord, calm with your soft hand
> The burning flames of her cheek.

YERMA.
> Listen to this pilgrim
> Travelling your holy path
> Forgive all her great sins.
> And open your rose
> Though it has a thousand thorns.

CHORUS.
> Lord, may the rose come in flower
> And may I not be left in darkness.

YERMA.
> On my fading flesh
> The miraculous rose.

They go in.

GIRLS *run on with long ribbons from the left, cross the stage, and run off again.*

Then another three GIRLS *enter from the right, also cross, and rush off again. There's a crescendo of voices, with the sounds of little bells and tambourines. High up on the stage seven* GIRLS *appear, waving their ribbons to the left. The noise grows louder and two folkloric figures enter, one representing the* MALE *and the other the* FEMALE. *They wear huge masks. The* MALE *carries a bull's horns in his hand. They are in no way grotesque, but of great beauty and communicate a sense of belonging to the ancient earth. The* FEMALE *shakes a collar of bells. The back of the stage fills up with a* CROWD *of people who shout and pass comments on the dance. Darkness is falling.*

BOY. The devil and his wife! The devil and his wife!

FEMALE.
In the river of the mountain
The sad wife was bathing.
Up her body went crawling
Sad snails of the water.
The sand on the riverbank
And the breezes of the mountain
Set fire to her laughter
And made her shoulders shake and shiver.
Oh, she was naked
She was very very naked
The sad wife in the water!

BOY. Oh, how sad she was! How sad!

MAN 1.
How dead withered flower
In the wind and the water!

MAN 2.
Tell the one who waits!

MAN 1.
Tell the one who's awaiting!

MAN 2.
Her with the dry belly
And the broken colour!

FEMALE.
When night comes I'll tell him
Under the clear dark night of sky
The night when the dry women gather
That's when I tear my skirt open.

CHORUS.
And at once the night falls!
The dark night was coming!
Look how black and dark it is getting
By the banks of the river in the mountain.

Guitars start to play.

MALE (*getting up and starting to wave his horns*).
How pale and wan is the lonely wife
How sad she is among the dead flowers!
But soon you will open your scarlet flowers
When the male unfolds his dark cloak.

He comes closer.

If you come to the church
To ask for your belly to ripen
Don't wear a veil of mourning
But a blouse of fine silk
Go alone behind the walls
Under the shade of the fig trees
And bear the weight of my earth body
From dusk till day's dawning.
Oh, how the moon shines
How bright the sun is shining!
And look how her hips are swaying.

FEMALE.
Crown her with flowers
Adorn her breasts with pure gold!

MALE.
Seven times was she moaning
In her joy and her delight
Seven times seven was there joining
Bright day and dark night.

MAN 1.
And the horn slips inside her!

MAN 2.

With the rose and the dance.

MAN 1.

Oh, how the wife is swaying!

MALE.

The male always rules
In this pilgrimage.
The husbands are bulls
And the male always governs,
And the pilgrims are flowers
For the men who can pick them.

BOY.

Let the air come inside her!

MAN 2.

Nail her with the branch!

MALE.

Come and see the pale woman
Now she's swimming in the fire.

MAN 1.

She's swaying like a reed.

BOY.

She's opening like a flower.

MEN.

Young girls should look elsewhere!

MALE.

The woman's body burns
The woman's body shines
And honour is scattered like ashes.

They go off dancing to the sound of handclaps and music. They are singing.

There are gardens in the sky
With rosebushes of joy
And among them all
The miracle of the rose.

Two GIRLS *pass across the stage again, shrieking. Enter the cheerful*
PAGAN OLD WOMAN.

OLD WOMAN. Who'll make more noise, I wonder. Will it be him or her, I wonder. Will we get any sleep, I wonder.

Enter YERMA.

You?

YERMA *is depressed. She says nothing.*

What are you doing here?

YERMA. I don't know.

OLD WOMAN. You don't believe in it? What about your husband?

YERMA *shows her exhaustion. She looks like someone whose mind is totally oppressed by some idea she cannot shift.*

YERMA. He's over there.

OLD WOMAN. What's he doing?

YERMA. Drinking. (*Pause. She takes her head in her hands and starts to cry.*)

OLD WOMAN. Less tears. More courage. I didn't want to say anything to you before. But I will now.

YERMA. What can you tell me that I don't know already!

OLD WOMAN. The one thing you can't go on ignoring. The thing that shouts from the rooftops. It's your husband who's to blame. Can you hear that? It's true what I'm saying. Or cut off both my hands. Neither his father, his grandfather or his great grandfather ever held themselves like real men. It's been a kind of miracle they've ever had children. They're made out of spit. But not your people. You have got brothers and cousins for miles all around. Look how great a curse has fallen on your beauty!

YERMA. Yes. A curse. A pool of poison in the fields.

OLD WOMAN. But you have legs. Use them. Walk out your house.

YERMA. Walk out?

OLD WOMAN. When I saw you in the pilgrimage my heart missed a beat. This is where the women come to meet new men and that's the Saint's miracle. My son's sitting behind the church waiting for me. My house needs a woman. Go with him and the three of us will live together. My son has real blood in his veins. Like me. If you come into my house it still smells of babies. The ash of your mattress will turn into bread and salt for your children. Come. Don't listen to what people say. As for your husband, I've got enough knives and castrating irons in my house to make sure he doesn't even dare cross the street.

YERMA. Quiet! Don't say another word! I could never do that. Do you imagine I could ever know another man? What do you think of my honour? Water cannot flow uphill. The moon cannot come out at midday. Go away. I'll keep following the path I'm on. Did you really imagine that I could go off with another man? That like a slave I would go begging for what's already mine? Know me better. Never talk to me again.

OLD WOMAN. Someone who's thirsty is grateful for water.

YERMA. I'm like a dried-up field where there's room for a thousand pairs of oxen. And what you offer me is a small glass of water from the well. Mine is a grief that does not reside in flesh.

OLD WOMAN (*fiercely*). Then go on like this. It's what you choose. Like thistles on a desert. Withered. Barren.

YERMA (*fiercely*). Yes. Barren. I know that. Barren. You don't have to rub my face in it. Don't be like one of those boys that take pleasure in the death agony of some little creature he's been tormenting. Since I got married I've been going round and round this word, but this is the first time I've heard it spoken, the first time anyone has ever said it to my face. The first time I see that it is true.

OLD WOMAN. I don't have any sympathy for you. None at all. I'll find my son another woman.

She goes. We hear a distant song sung by the pilgrims. YERMA *goes to the cart and* JUAN *appears from behind it.*

YERMA. Were you there?

JUAN. I was there.

YERMA. Were you listening?

JUAN. I was listening.

YERMA. And did you hear?

JUAN. Every word.

YERMA. Leave me alone and join the singing. (*She sits on some blankets.*)

JUAN. And now it's time I spoke.

YERMA. Then speak!

JUAN. And that I complain.

YERMA. Why?

JUAN. My throat is choked in bitterness.

YERMA. And it eats away my bones.

JUAN. I'm utterly beyond being able to deal with this endless lament for dark things, things outside life, things that only live in the air.

YERMA (*with total astonishment*). Outside life? Is that what you're saying? In the air?

JUAN. Things which have happened and which have nothing to do with either of us.

YERMA (*violently*). Go on! Go on!

JUAN. Things that don't matter to me. Do you hear me? Things that don't matter to me. I need to tell you. What matters to me is what I can hold in my hands. What I can see with my own eyes.

YERMA (*getting on to her knees in desperation*). Yes. Yes. That's what I needed to hear you speak. When the truth is locked inside, you can't see it, but how big it becomes, how much it matters when it is spoken out and lives in the open! And you think it doesn't matter! Now I've heard you say it!

JUAN (*getting close to her*). Think about it. That's how it has to be. Listen to me.

He embraces her to help her on her feet.

Many women would be so happy to live the way you do. Life is sweeter without children. I'm so happy not to have any. And we are not to blame.

YERMA. So what are you looking for in me?

JUAN. Your self.

YERMA (*excited*). Yes. That. You were looking for a home, peace and quiet, and a wife. But nothing else. Is it true what I'm saying?

JUAN. It's true. As everything.

YERMA. And what about the rest? What about your son?

JUAN (*angrily*). Didn't you hear me? I said it doesn't matter! Don't ask any more of me! Have I got to shout it in your ear to make you understand. To see if for just this once you could be at peace!

YERMA. And you've never thought about it when you've seen me desiring it?

JUAN. Never.

They are both on the ground.

YERMA. And there's no use me hoping?

JUAN. No.

YERMA. And what about you?

JUAN. Nothing. Get used to it!

YERMA. Barren!

JUAN. And living in peace. You with me, calmly, pleasantly. Embrace me! (*He embraces her.*)

YERMA. What do you want?

JUAN. You. You're so beautiful under the moon.

YERMA. You're looking at me like you're looking at a chicken. Or a sheep.

JUAN. Kiss me . . . Like this.

YERMA. No. Never. Never.

YERMA *lets out a cry and compresses her husband's neck. He falls backwards.* YERMA *continues to strangle him until he has died. The pilgrim's chorus starts to sing.*

Barren. Barren. Barren. But at least I know for sure. Now I absolutely know it for sure. And alone.

She gets up. PEOPLE *start to arrive.*

Now I can rest without ever having to wake up startled, wondering if there is new life in my blood. With a body barren for ever. What do you want to know? Keep away from me. I have killed my son. I have killed my own son!

A CROWD *gather who stay stock-still upstage. We hear the pilgrim's chorus.*

Curtain.

THE HOUSE OF BERNARDA ALBA

118

Characters

BERNARDA ALBA, *sixty years old*
MARÍA JOSEFA, *eighty years old, her mother*
ANGUSTIAS, *thirty-nine years old, her daughter*
MAGDALENA, *thirty years old, her daughter*
AMELIA, *twenty-seven years old, her daughter*
MARTIRIO, *twenty-four years old, her daughter*
ADELA, *twenty years old, her daughter*
LA PONCIA, *sixty years old, a servant*
MAID, *fifty years old*
PRUDENCIA, *fifty years old*
BEGGAR WOMAN
FIRST WOMAN
SECOND WOMAN
THIRD WOMAN
FOURTH WOMAN
GIRL
WOMEN IN MOURNING

The poet wishes to point out that these three acts are intended to be a photographic documentary.

ACT ONE

A blindingly white room inside BERNARDA ALBA's *house. The walls are thick. There are arched doorways with hessian curtains, edged with tassels and flounces. Cane chairs. On the walls are pictures of unlikely landscapes full of nymphs or legendary kings. It is summer. A heavy silence. We are deep in shadow. As the curtain rises, the stage is empty. We hear the tolling of a funeral bell.*

Enter the MAID.

MAID. Bloody bells! Going round and round my head!

LA PONCIA (*enters eating bread and chorizo*). Two hours of gibberish and they're still at it. And all to bury an old fart. May he rest in peace. The place is swarming with priests. Still. The church looks lovely. Magdalena fainted at the first paternoster.

MAID. Poor thing. She'll miss him.

LA PONCIA. She was the only one the old man cared about. Still. At least we got a minute to ourselves. I was hungry.

MAID. What if she saw you?

LA PONCIA. Herself? Domineering old bitch! You know, just because she's not eating, she'd like to see the rest of us die of hunger. Still. She can go to hell. I just felt like a sausage.

MAID (*with an anxious eagerness*). Could you give me something for my little girl?

LA PONCIA. Take a few beans. No one'll notice.

MARÍA JOSEFA (*within*). Bernarda!

LA PONCIA. Have you got her well locked up?

MAID. I turned both the keys.

LA PONCIA. You should have put the bolt across as well. That old dear can pick locks with her fingers.

MARÍA JOSEFA. Bernarda!

LA PONCIA (*shouts*). She's coming! (*To the* MAID.) You make sure everything's clean. If Bernarda finds one thing she can't see her face in she'll tear out the few hairs I've got left.

MAID. What a woman! What a woman!

LA PONCIA. She's like an empress. She who must be obeyed. Do you know what she'd like to do? She'd like to sit on your heart and slowly squeeze the life out of it. She'd take a whole year to do it, and she'd just sit there, like on a throne, just watching you gasping for air. She'd just sit and watch you and smile. Her cold cold smile. That cup's filthy.

MAID. I've been scrubbing all day. My hands are bleeding.

LA PONCIA. She wants her house to be the cleanest, her manners to be the nicest, herself to be the highest class. It's her husband I felt sorry for. I expect he's glad to be dead. Got shut of her anyway.

The bells stop ringing.

MAID. Has all the family come?

LA PONCIA. Just hers. His people came to see his corpse. They just filed in, crossed themselves, and filed out again. They can't stand the sight of her.

MAID. Have we got enough chairs?

LA PONCIA. Probably. If not, they'll just have to sit on the floor. You know, since her father died she's not let a soul into the house. It's her little empire, and she doesn't want anyone else to see it. Tight-fisted old bitch!

MAID. She's always been good to you.

LA PONCIA. Thirty years I've worked for her. Thirty years washing her sheets. Thirty years scrubbing her floors. Eating her leftovers. Up all night when she coughs. Spending days on end with my ears glued to the walls. Just so I could bring her back some titbit of gossip she could blackmail the neighbours with. Thirty years of my life given up to her. And we've no secrets from each other. She's like an open book to me. And I hate her guts. I'd like to tear out her eyes and nail them to the doorpost.

MAID. That's terrible.

LA PONCIA. But don't worry. I'm a good bitch. I'm like her little dog who barks when she tells me to and snaps at the heels of the beggars when she sets me onto them. I've worked for her all my life and my sons work her land and they're married but one day I'll have had enough. One day.

MAID. And then what?

LA PONCIA. And then I'll lock myself in a room with her and throw away the key. I'll spit in her face for a year and by the time I've finished with her she'll look like one of those lizards the little boys torment in the streets. The kind they pick up and pull the legs off one by one. Not that I envy her. All she's been left with is five ugly daughters with not a penny to their name. Except the eldest. Angustias. And the only reason she's got money is because she's the daughter of the first husband. And he was rich. As for the others, they've got loads of fancy needlework, loads of lace on their underskirts but nothing when she dies. Nothing but dry bread and sour grapes.

MAID. I wish I had what they've got.

LA PONCIA. All we've got is our hands to work with and a hole to be buried in.

MAID. That's all we have. All they ever let us have.

LA PONCIA (*at the glass cupboard*). This is filthy.

MAID. I've tried soaking it. I've tried scrubbing it. The stains won't come out.

The bells ring.

LA PONCIA. That'll be them finishing. I think I'll go and listen. The best bit's always at the end. And that priest's got a lovely voice. In the paternoster it just went up and up and up. Like water filling a jar. Course, he fluffed it in the end, but it was good while it lasted. The only one who could do a good 'Amen' was the old sacristan. Tronchapinos. I used to love to hear him. I remember him at my mother's funeral, may she rest in peace. He made the walls shake. It sounded like there was a wolf in the church. (*Imitating him.*) Ameeeeeeen! (*Starts to cough.*)

MAID. You'll strain your voice.

LA PONCIA. I'd rather be straining something else! (*Exits, laughing.*)

The MAID *cleans. Bells ring.*

MAID. Ding ding dong. Ding ding dong. God forgive him.

BEGGAR WOMAN (*with a child*). Glory be to God.

MAID. Ding ding dong. God give him peace.

BEGGAR WOMAN (*louder, and with a certain irritation*). Glory be to God!

MAID (*annoyed*). And on earth peace and goodwill!

BEGGAR WOMAN. I've come for the leftovers.

MAID. See that door? It leads out to the street. Today's leftovers are for me.

BEGGAR WOMAN. It's all right for you. You get paid. Me and my child get nothing. We're alone in the world.

MAID. So are the dogs. They're alone in the world too. Doesn't do them any harm.

BEGGAR WOMAN. But I always get the leftovers.

MAID. Get out of here. Who said you could come in? Get out. You've left dirty footmarks all over my clean floor.

They go. The MAID *cleans.*

This house. This house where they use olive oil to polish the floors. This house with its mahogany cupboards and its fancy chairs. With its fine linen and brass bedsteads. Just so we can live in mud huts with our one tin plate and worn-out spoon. I hope the day comes when it's all burnt to the ground!

The bells start to ring.

You and your bells! You in your walnut coffin with its gilt handles and silken ropes to carry it! You're just the same as us now. No better off than us. Antonio María Benavides. Lying there in your stiff collar and your creaky boots. That's the last time you touch me up behind the stable door.

From the back, WOMEN IN MOURNING *start to enter, two by two. They wear black headscarves, long black skirts, and carry black fans. They slowly enter until they fill the stage.*

(*Bursting into tears.*) Antonio María Benavides! You will never come through that door again! Never see these walls or eat bread at your own table! I loved you more than anyone else who served you. (*Tearing her hair.*) How can I live now you have gone?

The two hundred WOMEN *have all come in.* BERNARDA *appears with her five* DAUGHTERS. BERNARDA *leans on a stick.*

BERNARDA (*to the* MAID). Silence!

MAID (*crying*). Bernarda!

BERNARDA. Less tears. More work. The house is filthy. Everything should have been spotless for the mourners. Now get out. This is not your place.

The MAID *goes out, sobbing.*

The poor are like animals. They are not in the least like us.

FIRST WOMAN. The poor also feel pain.

BERNARDA. They forget it when they see a plate of beans.

GIRL (*timidly*). One must eat to live.

BERNARDA. At your age I never spoke in front of my elders.

FIRST WOMAN. Be quiet, girl.

BERNARDA. No one has ever had to teach me my manners. Sit.

They sit. Pause.

(*Loudly.*) Don't cry, Magdalena. If you must cry go and do it under the bed. Do you hear me?

SECOND WOMAN. Has the threshing started?

BERNARDA. Yesterday.

THIRD WOMAN. The sun is heavy as lead.

SECOND WOMAN. I've never known such heat.

Pause. They all fan themselves.

BERNARDA. Is the lemon juice ready?

LA PONCIA *enters with a big tray of little white glasses, which she hands out.*

LA PONCIA. Yes, Bernarda.

BERNARDA. Give some to the men.

LA PONCIA. I've given them theirs already. They're drinking it out in the yard.

BERNARDA. Make sure they go out the same way they came in. I don't want them in the house.

GIRL (*to* ANGUSTIUS). Pepe el Romano was there.

ANGUSTIAS. I saw him.

BERNARDA. She saw his mother. His mother was there. Not Pepe. She never saw Pepe and neither did I.

GIRL. But I thought…

BERNARDA. There was one man there. An old man. The widower of Darajalí. He was there. Standing next to your aunt. We all saw him.

SECOND WOMAN (*aside, in a low voice*). She's got a vicious tongue!

THIRD WOMAN (*aside, in a low voice*). Sharp as a razor!

BERNARDA. The only man women should look at in church is the priest. And only because he wears a skirt. To look at any other man is to act like a bitch on heat.

FIRST WOMAN (*aside, in a low voice*). She's half on heat herself.

LA PONCIA (*between her teeth*). And devious with it.

BERNARDA (*striking the floor with her stick*). God be praised.

ALL (*crossing themselves*). May He be blessed and praised for ever.

BERNARDA. May His servant rest in peace

With Angels and Archangels

And all the Holy Company of Heaven.

ALL. May he rest in peace.

BERNARDA. May St Michael watch over him

With his sharp and terrible sword.

ALL. May he rest in peace.

BERNARDA. May St Peter open doors to him

With the key that opens Heaven and closes Hell.

ALL. May he rest in peace.

BERNARDA. May he dwell with the souls of the blessed

and the little spirits who light up the fields.

ALL. May he rest in peace.

BERNARDA. With the souls who die in holy charity

With the souls who watch over land and sea.

ALL. May he rest in peace.

BERNARDA. God give eternal rest to your servant Antonio
María Benavides and give him the crown of your eternal glory.

ALL. Amen.

BERNARDA (*stands up and sings*). *Requiem aeterna dona eis, Domine.*

ALL (*on their feet and chanting a Gregorian chant*). *Et lux perpetua luceat
eis.*

They all cross themselves.

FIRST WOMAN. God give you health to pray for his soul.

They start filing out.

THIRD WOMAN. May you always have bread to bake in your
oven.

SECOND WOMAN. And a roof to shelter you and your children.

They all file past in front of BERNARDA *and exit. Exit*
ANGUSTIUS *through another door, which leads to the yard.*

FOURTH WOMAN. May each day bring you joy; each day be
like the day of your wedding.

LA PONCIA (*entering with a purse*). The men have collected this
money for you to pay the priest for prayers.

BERNARDA. Thank them and give them brandy.

GIRL (*to* MAGDALENA). Magdalena.

BERNARDA (*to* MAGDALENA, *who starts to cry*). Ssssshhhh.

She hits the floor with her stick. Almost everyone has left.

(*To those who have gone.*) Go back to your caves! Back to your
mud huts to criticise everything you've seen! I hope it's years
before you darken my doors again!

LA PONCIA. You've got no right to complain. The whole village came.

BERNARDA. Yes, they came. To fill the house with sweat of their underskirts and the poison of their tongues.

AMELIA. Mother, don't talk like that!

BERNARDA. There's no other way of talking. Not about this wretched little village, without a river. This village of wells, where you're afraid to drink the water in case it's been poisoned.

LA PONCIA. What a state they've left the floor in!

BERNARDA. They've trampled all over it like a herd of goats.

LA PONCIA *cleans the floor.*

Daughter, give me a fan.

ADELA. Here's one.

She gives her a round fan decorated with red and green flowers.

BERNARDA (*throwing the fan to the ground*). Is this a fan to give a widow? Fans must be black. Learn to respect your father's memory.

MARTIRIO. Take mine.

BERNARDA. Won't you be hot?

MARTIRIO. I am never hot.

BERNARDA. You will be. We will brick up the doors and board up the windows. We won't let in a breath of air from the street. That's what happened in my father's house and in my father's father's house. Mourning will last for eight years. You will spend your days sewing. I have twenty chests of linen you will sew into sheets. Magdalena can embroider them. They will be for your trousseaux.

MAGDALENA. It's all the same to me.

ADELA (*bitter*). If you don't feel like doing it, then don't bother. Ours won't get embroidered, that's all. And you might get a better husband.

MAGDALENA. It won't make any difference. I'll never get married, I know that. I'd do anything rather than that. I'd rather sweep the streets. Anything rather than sit day after day in this dark room.

BERNARDA. That is what it is to be a woman.

MAGDALENA. Then women are cursed.

BERNARDA. Cursed or not, you do as I say. No use running to your father now. He can't help you any more. Needle and thread for females. Mule and whip for the man. That is the fate of people of substance.

Exit ADELA.

MARÍA JOSEFA (*off*). Bernarda, let me out!

BERNARDA (*shouts*). Let her go!

Enter the MAID.

MAID. It was hard work holding her down. She may be eighty, but she's as strong as an ox.

BERNARDA. My grandmother was the same. Strength runs in the family.

MAID. I had to gag her this morning. I stuffed an old sack in her mouth to stop her shouting about the washing-up water you give her to drink and the dog food you give her to eat. She says that's all she gets.

MARTIRIO. She's wicked.

BERNARDA (*to the* MAID). Let her run about in the yard.

MAID. She insisted on opening her old trunk and getting out all her jewels. Now she's put them all on and she says she's going to get married.

The DAUGHTERS *laugh*.

BERNARDA. Stay with her. Make sure she doesn't go near the well.

MAID. Are you worried in case she throws herself in?

BERNARDA. No. But it's the one spot in the yard where the neighbours can see her.

Exit the MAID.

MARTIRIO. We're going to change.

BERNARDA. You may. But not your headscarves.

Enter ADELA.

Where's Angustias?

ADELA (*in a sarcastic tone of voice*). Peeking at the men through a crack in the gate.

BERNARDA. And what were you doing there, may I ask?

ADELA. I wanted to make sure the hens were safe.

BERNARDA. Besides, the men have gone.

ADELA (*nastily*). There was still a group of them hanging about.

BERNARDA (*furious*). Angustias! Angustias!

ANGUSTIAS (*coming in*). Do you want something?

BERNARDA. Who were you looking at?

ANGUSTIAS. No one.

BERNARDA. Do you think it decent for a woman of your class to go running after men the day of her father's funeral? Answer me! Who were you looking at?

Pause.

ANGUSTIAS. I… I was looking at…

BERNARDA. Who?

ANGUSTIAS. No one!

BERNARDA (*advancing on her with her stick*). You sweet-tongued liar!

BERNARDA *hits* ANGUSTIAS.

LA PONCIA (*running in*). Bernarda, calm down!

She holds BERNARDA *back from* ANGUSTIAS. ANGUSTIAS *cries.*

BERNARDA. All of you, get out!

They leave.

LA PONCIA. She shouldn't have done it, I know. It was bad. But I don't think she really understood. Still. I was shocked to see her sidling off to the yard! There she was behind the window listening to the men's talk. Filth, of course. None of it worth listening to.

BERNARDA. That's all they come to funerals for! (*With avid curiosity.*) What did they talk about?

LA PONCIA. Paca la Roseta. Last night they tied her husband to a cattle trough and took her off to the olive grove.

BERNARDA. Did she resist?

LA PONCIA. Her? She enjoyed it. They say she rode along with her breasts hanging out and Maximiliano was playing her like a guitar. It doesn't bear thinking about!

BERNARDA. And then what happened?

LA PONCIA. What had to happen. They all came back just before dawn. Her hair was loose and she wore a wreath of flowers.

BERNARDA. She is the only bad woman in the village.

LA PONCIA. That's because she doesn't come from here. She comes from far away. And all the men who went with her are strangers too. Men from here would never do a thing like that.

BERNARDA. Of course not. But they like to hear about it just the same. And talk about it. And drool over it too.

LA PONCIA. That wasn't the only thing they spoke about.

BERNARDA (*looking from side to side a little fearfully*). What else did they talk about?

LA PONCIA. I can't tell you. I'd be too ashamed.

BERNARDA. And my daughter heard it all?

LA PONCIA. Of course!

BERNARDA. She takes after her aunts. She's sweet and white and slimy and she's got eyes like a sheep. All she wants to do is flirt with any little tradesman who takes her fancy. God knows how one has to struggle to make sure one's people grow up half-decent! How one has to suffer to stop them running wild!

LA PONCIA. Your daughters give you precious little trouble. And they're surely old enough now to look after themselves. Angustias must be well over thirty.

BERNARDA. She's just thirty-nine.

LA PONCIA. Imagine that. And she's never had a boyfriend.

BERNARDA (*furious*). And why should she have? Why should any of them? They get on very well without!

LA PONCIA. I'm sure I never meant to hurt your feelings.

BERNARDA. There's no one within a hundred miles of here who can touch them. The men here are simply not of their class. Do you want me to hand them over to some farmhand?

LA PONCIA. You could have looked in another village.

BERNARDA. Oh yes, and sold them!

LA PONCIA. No, Bernarda. Not sold them. Married them . . . Of course, in other places it might be you who'd look poor!

BERNARDA. Shut that vicious mouth of yours!

LA PONCIA. It's impossible to talk to you. Do we or do we not trust each other?

BERNARDA. We do not. You work for me. I pay you. That is all!

MAID (*entering*). Here's the lawyer to sort out the will.

BERNARDA. I'm coming. (*To the* MAID.) You whitewash the yard. (*To* LA PONCIA.) And you pack away all the dead man's clothes.

LA PONCIA. Perhaps we could give some things away.

BERNARDA. No. Nothing. Not a button! Not even the handkerchief we used to cover his face!

She exits slowly, leaning on her stick, and as she leaves she suddenly turns back to look at her servants. They leave after her.

Enter AMELIA *and* MARTIRIO.

AMELIA. Did you take your medicine?

MARTIRIO. It won't do me any good.

AMELIA. But did you take it?

MARTIRIO. Yes, I took it. On time. Like I do everything. Like clockwork.

AMELIA. You've looked better since that new doctor came.

MARTIRIO. I feel just the same.

AMELIA. Did you see? Adelaida wasn't at the service.

MARTIRIO. That doesn't surprise me. Her husband won't even let her out the door. She used to be so cheerful. Now she's always miserable.

AMELIA. I used to think things got better when you had a man. Now I don't know any more.

MARTIRIO. It doesn't make any difference.

AMELIA. What makes it so bad is all this endless gossip. It never lets us live. Poor Adelaida. It's really made her suffer.

MARTIRIO. She's terrified of Mother. She's the only one who knows the story of her father. And every time Adelaida's come, Mother's stuck the knife in. Her father went to Cuba and killed a man so he could marry his wife. And then he left her to run off with this other woman who had a daughter. And when he got tired of the mother, he ran off with the daughter. The mother went mad. She killed herself and he married the daughter. And she's Adelaida's mother.

AMELIA. The man's a criminal. Why hasn't he been locked up?

MARTIRIO. Because men always stick up for each other. Because they always cover up things like this and none of them has the guts to speak out.

AMELIA. And anyway, it's not Adelaida's fault.

MARTIRIO. No, but history has a habit of repeating itself. That's all life is. Things repeating themselves. I can see it now. And what'll happen to her will be the same as what happened to her mother and her grandmother. And they were both her father's wives.

AMELIA. It doesn't bear thinking about.

MARTIRIO. It's better never to see a man. I've been afraid of them ever since I was a little girl. I used to watch them as they yoked the oxen or carried the sacks of corn. They always used to shout and kick. I was always afraid of growing up in case one of them suddenly picked me up in his arms. Anyway, God has made me weak and ugly and set them completely apart from me.

AMELIA. Don't say such things! Enrique Humanes was after you. He liked you.

MARTIRIO. That was something people made up! Once I stood in my shift at the window. I stood there all night, waiting. Someone had told me he was coming, but he never came. It had just been talk. And then he married someone else. Someone who had more money.

AMELIA. And who was ugly as sin!

MARTIRIO. That doesn't bother them! All they care about is their oxen and their land and some submissive little creature to cook their food.

AMELIA (*sighs*). You're right!

Enter MAGDALENA.

MAGDALENA. What are you doing?

MARTIRIO. Nothing special.

AMELIA. What about you?

MAGDALENA. I've been running. Running through the rooms of the house. Just to go somewhere. I wanted to see those old pictures our grandmother made. You remember. The embroidery poodle and the Negro wrestling with the lion. The ones we used to love so much when we were girls. Things were better then. Weddings used to last a fortnight. And no one ever gossiped. These days everyone is so much more polite. The brides wear white veils like they do in the cities and everyone drinks wine out of bottles. But now we're all petrified in fear of what the neighbours might say and just sit here and slowly rot.

MARTIRIO. What else can we do?

AMELIA (*to* MAGDALENA). You've left your shoelace undone.

MAGDALENA. So what?

AMELIA. You'll trip and you'll fall!

MAGDALENA. One less!

MARTIRIO. Where's Adela?

MAGDALENA. Oh. She's gone and put on her green dress. The one she was going to wear on her birthday, and she's run out into the hen run and is yelling: 'Hens! Hello, hens! Look at me! Look at me!' I had to laugh!

AMELIA. If Mother catches her!

MAGDALENA. Poor soul! She is the youngest of us and still has dreams! I'd give anything to see her happy.

Pause. ANGUSTIUS *walks across the stage with some towels in her hand.*

ANGUSTIAS. What time is it?

MARTIRIO. Twelve.

ANGUSTIAS. Already?

AMELIA. It's just struck.

Exit ANGUSTIUS.

MAGDALENA (*insinuatingly, meaning* ANGUSTIUS). Have you heard…?

AMELIA. Heard what?

MAGDALENA. Go on!

MARTIRIO. We don't know what you're talking about!

MAGDALENA. I'd better tell you then. But don't tell anyone. Keep your heads together like two little sheep, and don't breathe a word! The news about Pepe el Romano!

MARTIRIO. Ah!

MAGDALENA (*mimicking her*). 'Ah!' Pepe el Romano is going to marry Angustias. People are talking about it in the village. Yesterday he was hanging about the house and today, they say, he's going to send someone round.

MARTIRIO. I'm glad. He's a good man.

AMELIA. I'm glad too. Angustias deserves him.

MAGDALENA. You're not glad at all. Neither of you are.

MARTIRIO. Magdalena!

MAGDALENA. If I thought he was really coming for her sake, or was really attracted to her as a woman, then I would be glad. But he's coming for the money. We all know that. I mean, I know Angustias is our sister but we're all family too and we can talk honestly together. And you've got to admit that she is old and she is sickly and looks like a stick in a dress. No. That's wrong. That's what she looked like when she was twenty. In her prime. Now she looks like nothing on earth.

MARTIRIO. You shouldn't say such things. Good luck always comes to the one who least expects it.

AMELIA. No, she's right! Angustias is the only one who's rich. It's her father's money and she gets it now because our father is dead and they've got to divide the property. And that's why the men are after her.

MAGDALENA. Pepe el Romano is twenty-five years old and the best-looking man for miles around. The most natural thing – the most human thing! – would be for him to go after you, Amelia, or our Adela who's only twenty. What's wrong is for him to go after the oldest, the ugliest and the least attractive of us all. And anyway, she always talks through her nose.

MARTIRIO. Perhaps he likes that!

MAGDALENA. I could never stand your hypocrisy!

MARTIRIO. That's not fair!

Enter ADELA.

MAGDALENA. Did the hens admire you?

ADELA. What else am I supposed to do!

AMELIA. If Mother sees you she'll scratch your eyes out!

ADELA. I love this dress. I was going to wear it the day we went to the river. We were going to sit by the watermill and eat melons, and I was going to wear it. It would be the most beautiful dress in the world.

MARTIRIO. It is lovely!

ADELA. It really suits me too. It's the best one Magdalena has ever made me.

MAGDALENA. What did the hens think of it?

ADELA. They liked it so much they gave me a present. About four million fleas to hop all over my legs!

They laugh.

MARTIRIO. The best thing to do is dye it black.

MAGDALENA. The best thing to do is give it to Angustias. She can wear it when she marries Pepe el Romano!

ADELA (*trying to hide her feelings*). But Pepe el Romano…

AMELIA. Haven't you heard?

ADELA. No.

MAGDALENA. You must have.

ADELA. It can't be true!

MAGDALENA. Anything can be true. As long as you've got the money!

ADELA. So that's why he stayed behind after the funeral. And that's why he was looking through the bars of the gate… (*Pause.*) And that man is capable of…

MAGDALENA. Capable of anything. Anything at all.

Pause.

MARTIRIO. What are you thinking? Adela?

ADELA. I'm thinking this is the worst time in my life for me to have to go into mourning.

MAGDALENA. You'll get used to it.

ADELA (*bursting into tears of rage*). No, I won't get used to it! I refuse to get used to it! I don't want to be shut up in here. I don't want to go stale. I don't want to be like you! I don't want my flesh to go off! I'll get up tomorrow and put on my green dress and walk out the front door. I want out of here! I want out!

Enter the MAID.

MAGDALENA (*sternly*). Adela!

MAID. Poor girl! How she misses her father! (*Exits.*)

MARTIRIO. Be quiet!

AMELIA. It's the same for all of us!

ADELA *calms down.*

MAGDALENA. The maid almost heard you!

MAID (*appearing*). Pepe el Romano is coming down the street.

AMELIA, MARTIRIO *and* MAGDALENA *rush to the door.*

MAGDALENA. Let's go and see him!

Quick exit.

MAID (*to* ADELA). Aren't you going?

ADELA. No.

MAID. Once he's turned the corner you'll see him better from your room. (*Exits.*)

ADELA *stays onstage a moment, uncertain what to do. Then she quickly makes for her room. Enter* BERNARDA *and* LA PONCIA.

BERNARDA. How sordid a business this is!

LA PONCIA. The amount of money that's been left to Angustias!

BERNARDA. Yes.

LA PONCIA. And not nearly so much to the others.

BERNARDA. You've said that three times already. I didn't want to reply then, and I don't want to now. But no. Not nearly so much. A lot less. Don't remind me again.

Enter ANGUSTIUS, *with her face heavily made-up.*

Angustias!

ANGUSTIAS. Mother.

BERNARDA. How could you dare put that filth on your face? Today of all days. With your father hardly buried. How could you bear to even wash it?

ANGUSTIAS. He wasn't my father. Mine died long ago. Had you forgotten?

BERNARDA. You owe nothing to him. All he did was father you. But the man who fathered your sisters has made you a fortune!

ANGUSTIAS. That remains to be seen.

BERNARDA. Then out of decency! Out of respect!

ANGUSTIAS. Mother, can I go out now?

BERNARDA. Can you go out now? After I've taken the dirt off your face. Two-faced creature! Whore! The spitting image of your sluttish aunts!

She violently removes the make-up from ANGUSTIUS*'s face with a towel.*

Now get out!

LA PONCIA. Bernarda, you are going too far!

BERNARDA. My own mother may be mad but I have all my senses intact. I know exactly what I am doing.

Everyone comes in.

MAGDALENA. What's going on?

BERNARDA. Nothing.

MAGDALENA. If you're arguing over dividing the property, then don't worry. You're the richest and you're welcome to the lot.

ANGUSTIAS. Keep that tongue of yours locked up in its sty!

BERNARDA (*hits the floor with her stick*). Don't any of you think for a moment you're going to get the better of me! I am in command here and shall remain in command until they come to carry me out to my grave!

We hear shouts and cries and MARÍA JOSEFA, BERNARDA*'s mother, enters. She is incredibly old, garlanded with flowers on her head and and breast.*

MARÍA JOSEFA. Where's my mantilla? Bernarda, where is it? I don't want it to be yours. I don't want it to be anybody's. Not my mantilla, or my rings, or my beautiful black silk gown. None of you will ever marry. None of you! Bernarda, give me my necklace. Give me my pearls.

BERNARDA (*to the* MAID). Why did you let her in?

MAID (*trembling*). She managed to escape!

MARÍA JOSEFA. I escaped because I want to get married. I want to get married to a beautiful man. I'm going to get married to a beautiful man and live by the shores of the sea. By the sea. Not here. It's no use here. Men run away from women here.

BERNARDA. Mother, be quiet!

MARÍA JOSEFA. No, I won't be quiet, I'm tired of these spinster women, all desperate for men, with their hearts slowly crumbling into dust. I don't want to see them any more. I want to go back to my village, Bernarda, back to where I belong. I want a man to marry and be happy!

BERNARDA. Lock her up!

MARÍA JOSEFA. Don't lock me up, Bernarda! Don't lock me up! Let me go!

The MAID *seizes* MARÍA JOSEFA.

BERNARDA. Help her, all of you!

They all drag MARÍA JOSEFA *away.*

MARÍA JOSEFA. Let me go! Let me go! Bernarda! I want to get married! By the shores of the sea, by the shores of the sea!

Quick curtain.

End of Act One.

ACT TWO

White room inside BERNARDA's *house. Doors to the left lead to the bedrooms.* BERNARDA's DAUGHTERS *are sitting in chairs, sewing.* MAGDALENA *embroiders.* LA PONCIA *is with them.*

ANGUSTIAS. I've just finished the third sheet.

MARTIRIO. For the third daughter. Amelia: your sheet.

MAGDALENA. What shall I put on yours, Angustias? Shall I put on Pepe's initials too?

ANGUSTIAS (*curtly*). No.

MAGDALENA (*loudly*). Adela, are you coming?

AMELIA. She'll be in bed.

LA PONCIA. There's something wrong with that girl. She's always trembling. She's frightened of something. And she won't keep still. As if she had a lizard between her breasts.

MARTIRIO. She's just like the rest of us. She's got to put up with it.

MAGDALENA. All of us except Angustias.

ANGUSTIAS. And I'm fine, thank you very much, and anyone who doesn't like it will just have to explode.

MAGDALENA. You've always been noted for your tact.

ANGUSTIAS. Fortunately I am about to leave this hell.

MAGDALENA. Let's hope you never do.

MARTIRIO. That's enough, both of you!

ANGUSTIAS. Better to have gold in your chest than pretty eyes in your face!

MAGDALENA. It's all just going in one ear and out the other.

AMELIA (*to* LA PONCIA). Open the door a bit and let in some fresh air.

LA PONCIA *does so.*

MARTIRIO. Last night I was so hot I couldn't sleep a wink.

AMELIA. Me neither!

MARTIRIO. I had to get up to try and cool down. There was this great dark storm cloud in the sky and I could have sworn I felt a few drops of rain.

LA PONCIA. It was one in the morning. The earth breathed fire. I got up too. Angustias was still at the window with Pepe.

MAGDALENA (*ironically*). So late? What time did he go?

ANGUSTIAS. Why ask if you saw him yourself?

AMELIA. He must have left about half-past one.

ANGUSTIAS. How do you know?

AMELIA. I heard him cough and I heard the hooves of his mare.

LA PONCIA. But I heard him about four!

ANGUSTIAS. You can't have done.

LA PONCIA. I'm sure I did!

MARTIRIO. I thought I heard something too.

MAGDALENA. How very strange!

Pause.

LA PONCIA. Angustias, tell us what he said. Go on. What did he say the first time he came to your window?

ANGUSTIAS. Nothing special. What do you think he'd say? He just said… ordinary things. Things people say.

MARTIRIO. It really is the oddest thing. I mean, there's two people who don't know each other at all. Who've never even spoken to each other in their lives before. And suddenly there they are. At a window. Looking at each other through iron bars. About to get married.

ANGUSTIAS. But that's the way it's done. It's just normal. It doesn't feel a bit strange to me.

AMELIA. It would make me feel funny.

ANGUSTIAS. But it doesn't. Not when it happens. Because when a man comes up to you at the window it's all been settled already. He knows you've got to say yes.

MARTIRIO. Yes, but he's still got to ask.

ANGUSTIAS. Obviously!

AMELIA (*with avid curiosity*). Then what did he say?

ANGUSTIAS. He just said, 'You know I want you. I need a woman who's good, and well-behaved, and if you agree, that's you.'

AMELIA. Things like that make me feel ashamed!

ANGUSTIAS. Me too, but you just have to put up with them!

LA PONCIA. Is that all?

ANGUSTIAS. He said other things too. He did all the talking.

MARTIRIO. But what about you?

ANGUSTIAS. I couldn't say a word. I was too frightened. It was the first time I'd ever been alone with a man.

MAGDALENA. And such a handsome man too.

ANGUSTIAS. He's quite good-looking!

LA PONCIA. The things that happen when people start to know what they're doing! The things they say and do with their hands...! The first time my husband Evaristo el Colorín came to my window... (*Laughs.*)

AMELIA. What happened?

LA PONCIA. It was really dark. But I could see him coming. And when he got up to the window, he said, 'Good evening.' And then I said, 'Good evening,' and then we never said a word for half an hour. I was drenched in sweat. And then Evaristo came up to me, came up so close it was as if he wanted to squeeze between the bars and he said, in a very low voice, he said, 'Come here so I can feel you!'

They all laugh. AMELIA *suddenly breaks off and runs to listen at a door.*

AMELIA. Oh! I thought I could hear Mother coming.

MAGDALENA. She'd have skinned us alive!

They keep on laughing.

AMELIA. Ssssshhhh! She's going to hear us!

LA PONCIA. After that he behaved himself. He could have taken up all sorts of things, but instead he took up canaries. None of you are married, and when you are, the first thing you've got to learn is that after a fortnight your man'll get tired of making love. All he'll care about then is his stomach. And after a fortnight of that, all he'll care about is the nearest bar. And anyone who doesn't like it just has to go inside a corner and cry herself to pieces.

AMELIA. You didn't do that.

LA PONCIA. I could stand up to him!

MARTIRIO. Is it true you used to beat him?

LA PONCIA. Of course. I tell you, once I almost poked his eye out.

MAGDALENA. That's the way women should be!

LA PONCIA. I'm like your mother. One day he said something that really annoyed me and I killed all his canaries. I took the pestle and squashed their heads. It was something he said. Really got up my nose. I can't remember what it was now.

They all laugh.

MAGDALENA. Adela, don't miss this.

AMELIA. Adela.

Pause.

MAGDALENA. I'll go and see! (*Goes into her room.*)

LA PONCIA. That girl's ill!

MARTIRIO. What else do you expect? She hardly ever sleeps!

LA PONCIA. Then what does she do at night?

MARTIRIO. Do you really want to know?

LA PONCIA. You'll know better than me. You sleep next door.

ANGUSTIAS. She's eaten up by envy.

AMELIA. Don't exaggerate.

ANGUSTIAS. No, it's true. I can see it in her eyes. She's starting to look a bit mad.

MARTIRIO. Don't talk about madness. Not here. Don't even mention the word!

Enter MAGDALENA *with* ADELA.

MAGDALENA. I thought you'd have been asleep.

ADELA. I couldn't sleep. My body's gone bad.

MARTIRIO (*pointedly*). You don't get enough sleep at night.

ADELA. Maybe.

MARTIRIO. Well then?

ADELA (*fiercely*). Leave me alone! It's none of your business how much I sleep! What I do with my body is up to me!

MARTIRIO. We're just worried about you!

ADELA. Worried, were you? You're just nosey! Weren't you sewing? Well, get on with it. Sew! I wish I was invisible, so I could walk through this house without anyone asking me where I was going!

MAID (*entering*). Bernarda wants you. The man's come with the lace.

They exit. As she goes, MARTIRIO *stares at* ADELA.

ADELA. Don't look at me! With your dead eyes. Have mine if you like. They still shine. Or have my shoulders to straighten the crook in your back, only don't keep looking at me! Just don't look at me!

Exit MARTIRIO.

LA PONCIA. Adela, she's your sister. She's the one who loves you most!

ADELA. She follows me about everywhere. Sometimes she pokes her nose into my room to see if I'm asleep. She doesn't let me breathe. And she goes on about me all the time. All about my face, which will go old, and my body, which will go to waste. And she's wrong. She's wrong! I'll give my body to whoever I please!

LA PONCIA (*pointedly, in a low voice*). To Pepe, Adela?

ADELA (*startled*). What did you say?

LA PONCIA. You heard me!

ADELA. Be quiet!

LA PONCIA (*loudly*). Did you think I hadn't noticed?

ADELA. Keep your voice down!

LA PONCIA. Kill these dreams!

ADELA. How much do you know?

LA PONCIA. Where do you go when you get up at night? We can see you. See you go. We old women can see through walls.

ADELA. I wish you were blind!

LA PONCIA. I have twenty pairs of eyes. Eyes in my hands. Eyes in my feet. Eyes everywhere when I need them. And I need them now. Need them to keep track of what you and Pepe are up to. Though for the life of me I don't understand what you think you'll get from him just now. Why did you stand at the window the last time Pepe came? Why did you open the window and turn on the light? Why did you take off your clothes?

ADELA. It's not true!

LA PONCIA. Don't be like a baby! Leave your sister alone, and if you fancy Pepe then it's just too bad. You'll have to put up with it.

ADELA *cries.*

And anyway, who says you can't marry him? Your sister Angustias is an invalid. She won't survive her first child. She's old and sickly and she's got narrow hips and I can tell you she'll die. I know. Then Pepe will do what all widowers do round here: he'll marry the youngest and most beautiful sister. And that's you. Feed on that hope, and forget the rest. But don't break the law of God.

ADELA. Be quiet!

LA PONCIA. I won't be quiet!

ADELA. Mind your own business. Stop snooping!

LA PONCIA. I'll be closer to you than your own shadow!

ADELA. Why don't you just clean the house? Why don't you just go to bed at night and pray over all your dead bodies? Why do you have to stick your nose into other people's affairs? Snuffling about in the dirt like a sow!

LA PONCIA. I keep alert! I don't want people to spit as they pass this door.

ADELA. What's made you suddenly so fond of my sister?

LA PONCIA. I don't care about her at all. Not about her, not about any of you. I just don't want to live in a house of ill repute. I'm too old to get involved in dirt!

ADELA. It's too late. Anything you say is useless. I'll push you in the dirt and walk right over you. And I'll do the same to my mother. Anything to quench this fire that burns between my legs and in my mouth. But you've got nothing on me. What can you say against me? That I lock myself in my room and won't open the door? Nothing wrong with that! That I don't sleep? I'm not the only one! I'm cleverer than you! You'll see. I'm quick as a hare. Quicker! Just you see! I'll slip between your fingers!

LA PONCIA. Don't challenge me. Adela, don't challenge me! Nothing escapes me. Keep something dark, and I'll bring it to light! Hush something up, and I'll shout it out loud! I can set the bells ringing!

ADELA. Even if you took four thousand yellow flares and lit them in every corner of the yard, you still couldn't stop me. No one can. It has to happen, Poncia. Has to. No one can stop it.

LA PONCIA. You love him that much!

ADELA. That much! When I look into his eyes I feel like I'm drinking his blood. Drop by drop by drop!

LA PONCIA. I won't hear this!

ADELA. You'll hear it! I used to be scared of you. But no more. Now I am stronger than you!

Enter ANGUSTIUS.

ANGUSTIAS. Still talking!

LA PONCIA. She keeps insisting I go out in this heat and buy her some piece of nonsense from the shop.

ANGUSTIAS. Did you get me the perfume?

LA PONCIA. Yes. The most expensive in the shop. And the powder. I've put them on the table in your room.

Exit ANGUSTIUS.

ADELA. And hush!

LA PONCIA. We'll see!

Enter MARTIRIO, *carrying some pieces of lace,* AMELIA, *and* MAGDALENA.

MAGDALENA (*to* ADELA). Have you seen the lace?

AMELIA. Those pieces Angustias bought for her wedding sheets are just beautiful.

ADELA (*to* MARTIRIO). What are those for?

MARTIRIO. They're for me. For a petticoat.

ADELA (*sarcastically*). We all have our dreams!

MARTIRIO (*pointedly*). They're just for me. No one else. I don't need to display myself.

LA PONCIA. No one ever sees your petticoat.

MARTIRIO (*pointedly, looking at* ADELA). Sometimes people do! Besides, I love underwear. If I was rich, I'd have it all in silk. It's one of the few things I can still enjoy.

LA PONCIA. This kind of lace looks lovely on a baby's bonnet. Or a christening robe. I could never afford it for mine. I wonder if Angustias will use it for hers. She'll keep you sewing night and day if she takes it into her head to breed.

MAGDALENA. I don't intend to sew a single stitch. Not for her.

AMELIA. And I'm not going to look after anyone else's kids. Look at those people in the alley, run off their feet for four brats.

LA PONCIA. They're still better off than you. Things happen in their house. People hit each other. People laugh!

MARTIRIO. So why don't you work for them?

LA PONCIA. Because I'm stuck here, that's why. Stuck with this convent.

We hear little bells in the distance, as if through various walls.

MAGDALENA. It's the men going back to work.

MARTIRIO. In this sun!

LA PONCIA. It struck three a minute ago.

ADELA (*sitting down*). Oh, I wish I could go out to the fields!

MAGDALENA (*sitting down*). Each according to their class!

MARTIRIO (*sitting down*). That's how it is!

AMELIA (*sitting down*). Worse luck!

LA PONCIA. This time of year there is nowhere like the fields. Nowhere better. Yesterday morning the reapers came. Forty young men. Forty handsome young men.

MAGDALENA. Where have they come from?

LA PONCIA. Far away. From the mountains. They're full of joy! They sing and throw stones! And yesterday a woman came. She had sequins all over her dress and she danced to a tambourine. Twenty of them made a deal with her and took her to the olive grove. I watched them. The boy who hired her was firm and strong and had green eyes.

AMELIA. Is that true?

ADELA. It could be!

LA PONCIA. Years ago another came and I gave my son money to go with her. Men need these things.

ADELA. They're forgiven everything.

AMELIA. If you're a woman, you're punished just by being born.

MAGDALENA. We don't even own our eyes!

We hear a distant song getting closer and closer.

LA PONCIA. It's them. Singing. They have wonderful songs.

AMELIA. They are going out to reap.

SONG. The reapers go out in the fields,
Searching for the ears of the wheat,
What they find are the hearts of the girls,
Who fall in love with them when they meet.

We hear tambouines and drums. Pause. All listen in total silence, a silence pierced through and through by the heat.

AMELIA. Don't they care about the heat!

MARTIRIO. It licks them with tongues of fire.

ADELA. I'd like to be a reaper. To be free to come and go. To forget this longing.

MARTIRIO. What longing have you to forget?

ADELA. Everyone has something.

MARTIRIO (*with deep meaning*). Everyone.

LA PONCIA. Quiet! Quiet!

SONG (*very far away*). There's a girl behind each window,
    A girl behind each door,
    Open them and hand out roses,
    The reaper wants some more…

LA PONCIA. What a beautiful song!

MARTIRIO (*nostalgically*). There's a girl behind each window,
    A girl behind each door…

ADELA (*passionately*). Open them and hand out roses,
    The reaper wants some more…

    The sound goes further and further and further away.

LA PONCIA. Now they're turning the corner.

ADELA. Let's watch them from my room.

LA PONCIA. Don't open the window. Open it just a crack and they'll push it open wide.

    LA PONCIA, MAGDALENA *and* ADELA *go off.* MARTIRIO *stays behind. She remains sitting in a low seat with her head between her hands.*

AMELIA (*coming up to her*). What's wrong?

MARTIRIO. I can't stand the heat.

AMELIA. Is that really all?

MARTIRIO. I wish the rain would come. I wish it was November. I can't wait for the frosts. Anything except this endless summer.

AMELIA. It'll all pass and then come back again.

MARTIRIO. I know! (*Pause.*) What time did you get to sleep last night?

AMELIA. I don't know. I sleep like a log. Why?

MARTIRIO. No reason, I just thought I heard people in the yard.

AMELIA. Did you?

MARTIRIO. Very late.

AMELIA. Weren't you frightened?

MARTIRIO. No. I've heard it before.

AMELIA. We should be careful. Couldn't it have been the farmhands?

MARTIRIO. They don't come till six.

AMELIA. Perhaps it was the young mule that hasn't been broken in yet.

MARTIRIO (*through gritted teeth and with heavy irony*). That'll be right. The young mule that hasn't been broken in yet!

AMELIA. We should tell someone!

MARTIRIO. No! Not yet! Don't mention it to anybody! I could have just imagined it.

AMELIA. Maybe.

Pause. AMELIA *starts to go off.*

MARTIRIO. Amelia.

AMELIA (*at the door*). What?

Pause.

MARTIRIO. Nothing.

Pause.

AMELIA. Why did you call me?

Pause.

MARTIRIO. I don't know. I just did. I'd said it before I realised.

Pause.

AMELIA. You should go and lie down.

ANGUSTIUS *comes onstage furiously, so there is a great contrast between this scene and the previous silences.*

ANGUSTIAS. Where's the picture of Pepe I keep under my pillow? Who's taken it?

MARTIRIO. Not me.

AMELIA. Nor me. I'd never take it. Not even if he were a pin-up saint in silver. Which he isn't.

Enter LA PONCIA, MAGDALENA *and* ADELA.

ANGUSTIAS. Where's my picture?

ADELA. What picture?

ANGUSTIAS. The one you've taken from me.

MAGDALENA. You've got a nerve to say that!

ANGUSTIAS. It was in my room yesterday and it's not there now.

MARTIRIO. I expect it got up last night and went for a walk in the yard. Pepe loves the fresh air.

ANGUSTIAS. That's not funny! When I find it I'll tell Mother.

LA PONCIA. Don't tell anyone! I'm sure it'll turn up! (*Looking at* ADELA.)

ANGUSTIAS. I'd like to know which one of you has got it!

ADELA (*looking at* MARTIRIO). Someone's got it, I wonder who!

MARTIRIO (*ironically*). I wonder!

BERNARDA (*coming in with her stick*). What is the meaning of this scandalous noise? In this heat there should be nothing but silence! All the neighbours will have their ears glued to the walls!

ANGUSTIAS. Someone's taken my fiancé's picture.

BERNARDA (*fiercely*). Who was it? Who?

ANGUSTIAS. One of them!

BERNARDA. Which one? (*Silence.*) Answer me! (*Silence. To* LA PONCIA.) Search all their rooms. Look under their beds. This is what comes of my being so slack! But don't think you can get away from me. I'll come back to haunt you in your dreams! (*To* ANGUSTIUS.) Are you sure you didn't lose it?

ANGUSTIAS. Certain.

BERNARDA. You've had a good look for it?

ANGUSTIAS. Yes, Mother.

Everyone is standing in a painful silence.

BERNARDA. And now at the end of my life you give me this bitter pill to swallow. The most vicious blow a mother has ever had to endure. (*To* LA PONCIA.) Haven't you found it yet?

Enter LA PONCIA.

LA PONCIA. Here it is.

BERNARDA. Where did you find it?

LA PONCIA. It was…

BERNARDA. Don't be afraid to say.

LA PONCIA (*surprised*). It was between the sheets of Martirio's bed.

BERNARDA (*to* MARTIRIO). Is that true?

MARTIRIO. Yes. It's true!

BERNARDA (*going up to* MARTIRIO *and hitting her with the stick*). Insect! Despicable little thief! I'd like to squash you flat and wipe you off the soles of my feet! Little wretch!

MARTIRIO (*fiercely*). Mother, don't hit me!

BERNARDA. I'll hit you as much as I like!

MARTIRIO. Only because I let you. Now stop! Do you hear me?

LA PONCIA. Show more respect to your mother!

ANGUSTIAS (*grabbing* BERNARDA). Leave her. Please!

BERNARDA. There's not a single tear in her eyes.

MARTIRIO. I won't cry just to give you pleasure.

BERNARDA. Why did you take the picture?

MARTIRIO. Can't I play a joke on my own sister? What else should I want it for?

ADELA (*exploding with jealousy*). That was no joke. You've never played a joke on anybody. You had something very different in mind. Admit it. Something is burning you up. Admit it.

MARTIRIO. Keep your mouth shut and don't dare make me speak. Because if I do I'll tell something that'll make even the walls hide their heads in shame.

ADELA. There's something about malicious people. They just can't stop telling lies.

BERNARDA. Adela!

MAGDALENA. You've both gone mad.

AMELIA. You're infecting us with evil thoughts.

MARTIRIO. Others do worse.

ADELA. Until they go too far. Then they're stripped naked for the world to see and the river sweeps them away.

BERNARDA. Shameless girl!

ANGUSTIAS. I can't help it if Pepe el Romano finds me attractive.

ADELA. Not you. Your money!

ANGUSTIAS. Mother!

BERNARDA. Silence!

MARTIRIO. Your fields and olive trees.

MAGDALENA. They're right!

BERNARDA. I said silence! I could see this storm coming, but I didn't think that it would break so soon. What a hail storm of hatred you've made break on my heart! But I'm not finished yet. I'll forge five chains of steel to bind you tight. I'll bolt and I'll bar every door against you, every door in my father's house so not even the walls will know my shame! Now get out, all of you! Get out!

The DAUGHTERS *leave.* BERNARDA *sits down, desolate.* LA PONCIA *is standing, leaning against a wall.* BERNARDA *suddenly strikes the floor with her stick and says:*

I will have to make them feel the weight of my hand! That is your duty, Bernarda. Your duty. And don't you forget it.

LA PONCIA. May I speak?

BERNARDA. Speak. I am sorry you heard. A stranger should never be allowed into a family's heart.

LA PONCIA. It can't be helped. I have seen what I have seen.

BERNARDA. Angustias must marry at once.

LA PONCIA. Obviously, you have to get her out of here.

BERNARDA. Not her. Him!

LA PONCIA. Him, yes. Obviously. You have to get him out of here! You're right to think that.

BERNARDA. I don't think. There are some things that cannot and should not be thought. I order.

LA PONCIA. And do you think he'll want to go?

BERNARDA (*standing up*). What's going on in that head of yours?

LA PONCIA. Nothing. He'll marry Angustias. Obviously.

BERNARDA. You've got something vicious hidden up your sleeve. I can tell. I know you too well. You can't wait to stick the knife in. Speak.

LA PONCIA. I don't want to stick the knife in. I just want to help. Helping and murdering aren't quite the same thing. I'm surprised you haven't noticed.

BERNARDA. Are you trying to warn me of something?

LA PONCIA. I don't blame you, Bernarda. I'm not accusing anyone. All I'm saying is this: look about you. Open your eyes.

BERNARDA. And what do you think I'll see?

LA PONCIA. You've always kept your eyes open. You've been able to see other people's faults from miles off. I've often thought you could read people's minds. But now you've gone blind. All of a sudden. Still, I suppose one's own family is something else altogether.

BERNARDA. Are you talking about Martirio?

LA PONCIA. Yes, if you like, Martirio… (*Curiously.*) Why should she have wanted to hide the picture?

BERNARDA (*wanting to make excuses for her daughter*). She said herself it was just a joke. What else could it have been?

LA PONCIA (*sarcastically*). You really think so?

BERNARDA (*vehemently*). I don't think so. I know!

LA PONCIA. That'll be right then. It's your family. You know best. But would it still be a joke if it was one of the neighbours?

BERNARDA. Now you're starting to stick the knife in.

LA PONCIA (*still with a cruel edge to her voice*). No, Bernarda. I wouldn't want to do that. It's just that something very big is happening here. I don't want to blame you for it, but you've never given your daughters any freedom at all. You can say what you like, but Martirio... is just desperate to fall in love. With anybody. Why didn't you let her marry Enrique Humanes? Why was it that the very day he was going to see her you sent him a message forbidding him to come?

BERNARDA (*fiercely*). And if I had to I'd do it again! And again and again! No one in my family marries the Humanes while I've got breath in my body! His father was a common labourer.

LA PONCIA. You and your airs!

BERNARDA. If I have airs it's because I've a right to them. And if you don't it's because of where you sprang from.

LA PONCIA (*with hatred*). Don't remind me! I'm too old for that. And I've always been grateful for your support.

BERNARDA (*pompously*). It doesn't sound like it!

LA PONCIA (*with her hatred hidden in gentleness*). Martirio will get over this.

BERNARDA. And if she doesn't, so much the worse for her! I don't think that is the 'very big thing' that is going on here. According to you. Nothing is going on here. And if anything did ever 'go on', you can be sure that word of it would never go beyond these walls.

LA PONCIA. I wouldn't be so sure! Other people in the village can also read people's minds. You're not the only one.

BERNARDA. How you'd love to see me and my daughters on the road to the brothel!

LA PONCIA. No one can predict where they might end up!

BERNARDA. I know where I'll end up! And my daughters! The brothel is the place for a certain woman who's already dead...

LA PONCIA (*fiercely*). Bernarda, have respect for my mother's memory!

BERNARDA. Then don't torment me with your wicked thoughts!

Pause.

LA PONCIA. I'd be better not getting involved.

BERNARDA. Exactly. Don't get involved. Keep your mouth shut. Do your work. That is the duty of the employee.

LA PONCIA. But I can't. I mean… don't you think that Pepe would be better married to Martirio, or even – better still! – to Adela?

BERNARDA. No.

LA PONCIA (*deliberately*). Adela. Now there's the proper wife for Pepe!

BERNARDA. Things never work out the way we'd like them to.

LA PONCIA. But it's hard to twist them from their proper course. I think it's wrong for Pepe to marry Angustias, and I'm not the only one. Other people think so too. It's in the air. And who knows what it may lead to in the end!

BERNARDA. There you go again! You're going out of your way to fill my mind with nightmares. I'm not going to listen to you, which is just as well. Because if I did, and if I really came to fully understand everything you are hinting at, I'd have to scratch out your eyes.

LA PONCIA. I wouldn't let you get near them!

BERNARDA. Fortunately I have my daughters' respect. And I have always had their obedience!

LA PONCIA. Oh yes, their obedience! Release them from that, and they'd be flying over the rooftops!

BERNARDA. I'd climb up myself and bring them down with grappling irons.

LA PONCIA. You were always strong!

BERNARDA. I can take care of myself!

LA PONCIA. But how things have changed! Even at her age, you should see how keen Angustias is over her man! He seems dead keen too! My eldest son told me that as he was going by with his oxen at dawn, they were still at it together. At four in the morning!

BERNARDA. At four in the morning!

ANGUSTIAS (*entering*). It's a lie!

LA PONCIA. That's what my son told me.

BERNARDA. Tell me the truth!

ANGUSTIAS. For more than a week now, Pepe has been leaving at one. God kill me if I lie.

MARTIRIO (*entering*). I also heard him leave at four.

BERNARDA. But – did you see him?

MARTIRIO. I didn't want to lean out of the window. Don't you meet now at the window that gives onto the alleyway?

ANGUSTIAS. He comes to my bedroom window.

ADELA *appears at her door.*

MARTIRIO. Then…

BERNARDA. What are you hinting at?

LA PONCIA. If you find out, you'll regret it! One thing's for sure: that Pepe was talking to someone at four in the morning. Someone who lives in your house.

BERNARDA. Do you know that for sure?

LA PONCIA. In this life, one can't ever be sure.

ADELA. Mother, don't you listen to someone who just wants to defame us all.

BERNARDA. I'll find out what I need to! And if people in the village want to throw slanders at me, I'll stand there like flint and dash them to pieces! We won't talk of this again. Sometimes people want to dig a pit of filth and push us into it to drown there.

MARTIRIO. I don't like to tell lies.

LA PONCIA. There must be something to it.

BERNARDA. There's nothing in it! I was born with my eyes wide open! Now I'll never shut them till the day I die.

ANGUSTIAS. But I've got a right to find out the truth.

BERNARDA. You've a right to nothing but obedience! And I'll have no one giving the orders here but me! (*To* LA PONCIA.) And you just stick to your job. And remember, all of you: I'm watching every step you take. Every little thing you do, I'll know all about it.

MAID (*entering*). There's a great crowd at the top of the street and all the neighbours are at their doors!

BERNARDA (*to* LA PONCIA). Run and find out what's going on!

Everyone starts to make for the door.

And where do you think you're going? I might have known you'd be the kind of women to hang about at windows and have no respect for their dead! Get back inside!

They exit, and so does BERNARDA. *We can hear distant shouts. Enter* ADELA *and* MARTIRIO, *who stay for a moment listening, without daring to take another step towards the front door.*

MARTIRIO. You're lucky I didn't talk!

ADELA. I could have spoken too.

MARTIRIO. And what could you have said? I've done nothing!

ADELA. Just because you haven't dared to. It takes guts to get anything done, and you haven't got it in you. No, you haven't done anything. You've just wanted to.

MARTIRIO. You can't go on like this for long.

ADELA. I'll have him all to myself!

MARTIRIO. I'll break it up.

ADELA (*pleading*). Martirio, let me be!

MARTIRIO. Never!

ADELA. He wants me to live with him!

MARTIRIO. I've watched him kiss you!

ADELA. I didn't want to. Not at first! I just felt tied to him. At the end of a chain! And he just dragged me towards him. I couldn't help it!

MARTIRIO. You'd be better off dead!

MAGDALENA *and* ANGUSTIUS *poke their heads round their doors. We can hear the tumult rising.*

LA PONCIA (*entering with* BERNARDA). Bernarda!

BERNARDA. What's happening?

LA PONCIA. La Librada's unmarried daughter had a son and no one knows its father.

ADELA. She had a son?

LA PONCIA. And she killed it to hide her shame. She buried it under some stones. The dogs found it. It was as if they had more heart than her. They pulled it out and God guided them to her door. That's where they left it. On her threshold. Now everyone wants to kill her. They're dragging her down the street, and the men are coming running through the fields, shouting so loud they're shaking the trees.

BERNARDA. Good. Let them come. Let them come with sticks and with heavy stones and beat her to death.

ADELA. They mustn't kill her. They mustn't.

MARTIRIO. Oh, but they must. Let's go out to watch.

BERNARDA. Let her pay the penalty for her shame.

We hear a woman scream outside. The tumult grows.

ADELA. Let her go free! Don't go outside!

MARTIRIO (*looking at* ADELA). Let her pay for what she's done!

BERNARDA (*at the front door*). Kill her before the police come! Heap her with burning coals in the place of her sin!

ADELA (*clutching her belly*). No! No!

BERNARDA. Kill her! Kill her!

Curtain.

End of Act Two.

ACT THREE

The inner courtyard of BERNARDA'*s house. The walls are white with a hint of blue. It is night-time. The decor needs to be utterly simple. The doorways are lit from the rooms within and give the stage a feeble glow of light.*

In the centre is a table lit by an oil lamp, where BERNARDA *and her* DAUGHTERS *are eating.* LA PONCIA *serves them.* PRUDENCIA *is sitting on her own.*

The curtain rises in the midst of profound silence, broken only by the clatter of crockery and the sounds of knives and forks.

PRUDENCIA. I must go, I've been here far too long.

BERNARDA. Don't go. We hardly ever see each other.

PRUDENCIA. Have they rung for the last rosary?

LA PONCIA. Not yet.

  PRUDENCIA *sits down.*

BERNARDA. And how's your husband?

PRUDENCIA. The same.

BERNARDA. We never see him, either.

PRUDENCIA. You know how he is. Ever since he quarrelled with his brothers over the inheritance, he's never been out the front door. He takes a ladder and climbs out over the walls.

BERNARDA. There's a real man for you. And how is he with your daughter?

PRUDENCIA. He has never forgiven her.

BERNARDA. Quite right. She is an enemy now. A daughter who disobeys is a daughter no more.

PRUDENCIA. I'd rather let things be. My only consolation is to go to church. But I'll have to stop going now. My sight's fading, and the boys are beginning to torment me. So hateful to be the sport of urchins.

We hear a heavy blow, as if something is striking the walls.

What was that?

BERNARDA. The stallion. He must be kicking the wall. We locked him up in the stable. He'll be feeling the heat. (*Shouts.*) Hobble it and let it out in the yard!

PRUDENCIA. Will you give him the new fillies?

BERNARDA. At dawn.

PRUDENCIA. And your herd's so big already. You've done terribly well.

BERNARDA. I've worked and suffered for it.

LA PONCIA (*butting in*). She's got the best stock for miles around! Pity the price has fallen.

BERNARDA. Would you like some cheese and honey?

PRUDENCIA. I have no appetite.

We hear the blow again.

LA PONCIA. For the love of God!

PRUDENCIA. It gave me such a fright! It sent shivers up my spine.

BERNARDA (*getting up angrily*). Have I got to tell you everything twice? Let him out so he can roll in the hay! (*Pause. As if speaking to the labourers.*) Then shut the fillies in the stable! But let him go free. Or else he'll kick the walls down. (*Goes back to the table and sits down again.*) What a life!

LA PONCIA. Toiling away like a man.

BERNARDA. That's how it is.

ADELA gets up from the table.

Where are you going?

ADELA. To get a drink of water.

BERNARDA (*loudly*). Bring a jug of cool water. (*To* ADELA.) You can sit down now.

ADELA sits down.

PRUDENCIA. And when will Angustias be married?

BERNARDA. His family are coming to arrange it in three days.

PRUDENCIA. You must be so happy!

ANGUSTIAS. Yes!

AMELIA (*to* MAGDALENA). Now you've spilt the salt!

MAGDALENA. Your luck can hardly get any worse. It's bad enough already.

AMELIA. It's still a bad sign.

BERNARDA. Nonsense!

PRUDENCIA (*to* ANGUSTIUS). Has he given you a ring?

ANGUSTIAS. Yes. Look. (*Shows it.*)

PRUDENCIA. Pearls. How lovely. But in my day, pearls meant tears.

ANGUSTIAS. But now things have changed.

ADELA. I don't agree. Things don't change their meaning. Engagement rings should be made of diamonds.

PRUDENCIA. That would be more proper.

BERNARDA. Pearls or diamonds, it's all the same. It doesn't matter. What matters is that things turn out the way one intends.

MARTIRIO. Or the way God ordains them.

PRUDENCIA. They tell me the furniture is beautiful.

BERNARDA. It should be. It cost me sixteen thousand reales.

LA PONCIA. I'll tell you what's best of all. The wardrobe. It's got a full-length mirror.

PRUDENCIA. I've never seen a wardrobe.

BERNARDA. In my day we used a chest.

PRUDENCIA. The main thing is for everything to turn out well.

ADELA. And that is something no one can predict.

BERNARDA. There is no reason to imagine otherwise.

We hear bells ringing a long, long way off.

PRUDENCIA. The last bell. (*To* ANGUSTIUS.) I must come back so you can show me your dress.

ANGUSTIAS. Whenever you wish.

PRUDENCIA. God give us all a good night's rest.

BERNARDA. Goodbye, Prudencia.

THE FIVE DAUGHTERS (*together*). May you go with God.

Pause. Exit PRUDENCIA.

BERNARDA. The meal is over.

All stand up.

ADELA. I'm going to the yard to stretch my legs and get a breath of fresh air.

MAGDALENA *sits on a low seat, leaning against the wall.*

AMELIA. Me too.

MARTIRIO. And me.

ADELA (*with suppressed hatred*). I'm hardly likely to get lost.

AMELIA. At night it's best not to be alone.

They exit. BERNARDA *sits down and* ANGUSTIUS *clears the table.*

BERNARDA. You must make it up with your sister. I've told you once already. I don't want to have to tell you again. What happened over the picture was a joke and you should forget all about it.

AMELIA. Martirio doesn't love me.

BERNARDA. I'm not concerned with feelings. What people feel is their own affair. What matters is the way things look. Harmony in the family. That's what concerns me. Do I make myself clear?

ANGUSTIAS. Yes, Mother.

BERNARDA. Then there's nothing else to be said.

MAGDALENA (*half-asleep*). Anyway, you'll soon be gone.

She sleeps.

ANGUSTIAS. Not soon enough for me.

BERNARDA. What time did you and Pepe finish last night?

ANGUSTIAS. Half-past twelve.

BERNARDA. And what does Pepe have to say for himself?

ANGUSTIAS. I don't know. He's always so distracted. He always seems to be thinking of something else and when I ask him what's on his mind, he just says, 'Men's affairs.'

BERNARDA. You should never have asked. Not now, and certainly not when you're married. Don't look at him unless he looks at you first. And speak only when you're spoken to. That way you'll have no trouble.

ANGUSTIAS. I think he's hiding something from me.

BERNARDA. Don't try to find out what it is. Never ask him. Above all, never let him see you cry.

ANGUSTIAS. I know I should feel happy, but I just feel wretched.

BERNARDA. If you should be happy then you are happy. They are one and the same.

ANGUSTIAS. I want to know him better. I look at him as hard as I can but he just gets all blurred. And all I see through the bars of my window is this shadow who seems shrouded in dust.

BERNARDA. That's just weakness. You'll get over it.

ANGUSTIAS. I hope so!

BERNARDA. Is he coming tonight?

ANGUSTIAS. No. He said he and his mother were going to town.

BERNARDA. Good. We'll all get an early night. Magdalena!

ANGUSTIAS. She's fast asleep.

Enter ADELA, MARTIRIO *and* AMELIA.

AMELIA. How dark it is out there!

ADELA. You can hardly see two paces in front of you.

MARTIRIO. A good night for robbers. And for liars.

ADELA. The stallion was standing in the middle of the yard. He was so white! He seemed to fill the darkness.

AMELIA. I was frightened. It looked like a ghost.

ADELA. There are stars in the sky as big as my fist.

MARTIRIO. She was staring at them so hard she almost cricked her neck. If she'd stared at them much more, her head would have snapped off.

ADELA. Don't you like the stars?

MARTIRIO. No. I don't care for them at all. Why should I? There's enough going on inside.

ADELA. That just about sums you up.

BERNARDA. You see things one way; she sees them another. She's got a right to.

ANGUSTIAS. Goodnight.

ADELA. Off to bed already?

ANGUSTIAS. Yes. Pepe is not coming tonight. (*Exits.*)

ADELA. Mother, why is it that whenever people see a flash of lightning or a shooting star they say 'God bless St Barbara, God's writing in the sky'?

BERNARDA. In the old days people knew things that have now been forgotten.

AMELIA. I hate shooting stars. I don't want to see them. I'd rather close my eyes.

ADELA. I love them. Just think of it: a desolate patch of sky, where everything's been quiet and dead for millions and millions of years and then suddenly – phweeeee! A shooting star.

MARTIRIO. But that's got nothing to do with us.

BERNARDA. So it's better not to think of it.

ADELA. It's so beautiful tonight. And the air is fresh and cool. I'd like to stay up all night to enjoy it.

BERNARDA. It's time we were all in bed. Magdalena!

AMELIA. Still fast asleep.

BERNARDA. Magdalena!

MAGDALENA (*crossly*). Leave me alone!

BERNARDA. Go to bed!

MAGDALENA (*getting up bad-temperedly*). Can't a body get a moment's peace? (*Goes off grumbling.*)

AMELIA. Goodnight. (*Exits.*)

BERNARDA. And you go too.

MARTIRIO. Why isn't Pepe coming?

BERNARDA. He went on a journey.

MARTIRIO (*looking at* ADELA). Oh, did he!

ADELA. See you tomorrow. (*Exits.*)

MARTIRIO *has a drink of water and exits slowly, staring at the doorway to the yard. Enter* LA PONCIA.

LA PONCIA. Are you still up?

BERNARDA. Enjoying the peace and quiet. Strangely enough, I don't see any trace of this 'very big thing' that you're so sure is going on.

LA PONCIA. Don't let's talk about it.

BERNARDA. Nothing happens here without my knowing all about it. Nothing at all. And that's because I keep watch.

LA PONCIA. You're right. Nothing is going on here. Looked at from outside. Your daughters are quiet and smile like porcelain dolls. And, oh yes, they live very quietly inside their glass cases. But neither you nor I nor anyone else can tell what's going on inside their minds.

BERNARDA. My daughters breathe easy.

LA PONCIA. All that is your business. You are their mother. I just look after the house. That's quite enough for me.

BERNARDA. You've changed your tune.

LA PONCIA. I know my place and I'm better off staying there.

BERNARDA. The truth is, you've nothing to say. There's no dirt for you to stir. If there was, you'd have stirred it up and invited all the neighbours in to watch.

LA PONCIA. I know more than you imagine.

BERNARDA. Does your son still see Pepe at four in the morning? Do the neighbours still go on and on repeating their silly little slanders against us?

LA PONCIA. No one says a word.

BERNARDA. Because there is nothing for them to say. There's no flesh for them to sink their teeth into. And all because I keep watch!

LA PONCIA. I won't tell you what I know because I'd be frightened of how you'd take it. But I'll tell you this: don't be so sure of yourself.

BERNARDA. I have every right to be sure!

LA PONCIA. A bolt of lightning could strike you dead! Your blood could clot and stop your heart beating!

BERNARDA. Nothing of the kind will happen here. Insinuate all you like; it won't make any difference. I'm on the alert. I'm on my guard.

LA PONCIA. So much the better for you.

BERNARDA. Naturally!

MAID (*entering*). I've done the washing up. Is there anything else, Bernarda?

BERNARDA (*standing up*). Nothing. I am going to my bed.

MAID. What time shall I wake you?

BERNARDA. Don't wake me at all. Tonight, I'm going to get a good night's sleep. (*Exits.*)

LA PONCIA. When you can't move a mountain, you're better off turning your back on it. Then at least you don't have to look.

MAID. She's so proud she just won't see. It's like she's tied a bandage round her own eyes.

LA PONCIA. There's nothing I can do. I wanted to head things off but now they frighten me. Hear that silence? It's the quiet before the storm. And it's brewing in each one of those rooms. When it breaks we'll all be swept away. But I've said all I could. What else can you do?

MAID. She's just so determined and she thinks everyone should be the same. She just won't understand the effect one man can have on a group of single women.

LA PONCIA. I don't blame Pepe. I don't think it's altogether his fault. It's true that he was after Adela a year or so ago and she was mad about him, but now she should have known her place and left him alone and not provoked him. He can't control himself. He's only a man.

MAID. Some people say he's spoken to Adela night after night.

LA PONCIA. They're right. (*Lowering her voice.*) And not just spoken to her either.

MAID. I dread to think what's going to happen.

LA PONCIA. This is a house at war. I'd like to sail across the sea and leave it right behind.

MAID. And all Bernarda does is hurry up the wedding and hope everything will be all right. I suppose she could be right.

LA PONCIA. No. Things have gone too far. Adela's got her mind set on something and the others watch and watch and never rest.

MAID. Even Martirio?

LA PONCIA. Especially Martirio. She's the worst of all. She's a poisoned well. She knows she'll never get Pepe herself and, rather than leave him to someone else, she'd rather kill the lot of them.

MAID. They're all as bad as each other.

LA PONCIA. They are women without men, that's all. And when it comes to sex, everything else gets swept away. Even ties of blood. Ssssshhhh. (*Listens.*)

MAID. What's going on?

LA PONCIA (*gets up*). The dogs are barking.

MAID. There must be someone in the yard.

Enter ADELA *in petticoat and bodice.*

LA PONCIA. Haven't you gone to bed?

ADELA. I want a drink of water. (*Drinks from a glass on the table.*)

LA PONCIA. I thought you were asleep.

ADELA. I was woken by thirst. Why aren't you in bed?

MAID. We're just going.

Exit ADELA.

LA PONCIA. Come on.

MAID. I'm worn out, Bernarda's kept me on my feet all day.

LA PONCIA. You take the light.

MAID. The dogs are going off their heads.

LA PONCIA. They won't let us get a wink of sleep.

They exit. The stage is almost dark. Enter MARÍA JOSEFA *with a lamb under her arm.*

MARÍA JOSEFA. My baby is a little lamb,
    I'll take him to the shore,
    I'll give him my breast and bits of ham,
    A little ant will sit at our door.
    Bernarda has a leopard face,
    Magdalena's a hyena,
    Little baby, little lamb,
    Baa, baa.
    Let's go to the stable at Bethlehem.
    (*Laughs.*) The door will open all on its own,
    And we'll go and we'll sit by the sea,
    We'll build a little hut like an orange pip,
    And we'll live there for ever, you and me.
    Bernarda has a leopard face,
    Magdalena's a hyena,
    Little baby, little lamb,
    Baa, baa.
    Let's go to the stable at Bethlehem.

She goes off, singing. Enter ADELA. *She cautiously looks about her, one way, and then the other, and then goes out into the yard. Enter* MARTIRIO *through another door. She stays centre stage, anxiously watching. She also wears bodice and petticoat, and round her shoulders is a little black shawl. Enter* MARÍA JOSEFA *from in front of her.*

MARTIRIO. Grandmother, where are you going?

MARÍA JOSEFA. Why won't you open the door?

MARTIRIO. What are you doing here?

MARÍA JOSEFA. Escaping. Who are you?

MARTIRIO. Go back to bed.

MARÍA JOSEFA. I know you. You're Martirio. Martirio with a martyr's face. Why don't you have a baby? I've got one. Look.

MARTIRIO. It's a sheep.

MARÍA JOSEFA. I know perfectly well it's a sheep.

MARTIRIO. Where did you get it from?

MARÍA JOSEFA. Why can't a sheep be a baby? Better to have a sheep than to have nothing at all. Bernarda's got a leopard's face, Magdalena's a hyena.

MARTIRIO. Not so loud!

MARÍA JOSEFA. You're right. It's very dark. Just because I've got white hairs you think I can't have a baby. But you're wrong there. I'll have baby after baby after baby. One baby will have white hair and then it'll have another baby and another and another. We'll all have babies and snow-white hair and we'll be like the waves of the sea: one after another after another after another. And then we'll all sit down and we'll all have white hair and we'll be like the foam of the sea. But not here. There's no foam here. Why's it all so dark? It's all so dark here. Everyone wears black. Everyone's always in mourning.

MARTIRIO. Be quiet!

MARÍA JOSEFA. When my neighbour had a baby, I brought her chocolate. And then she brought me some and I brought her some more and then she brought me more and so it went on and on and on for ever and ever. You'll have white hair but no one's ever going to bring chocolate to you. I've got to go, but all the dogs keep barking. I'm afraid of the dogs. They might bite me. Will you help me? I want to leave the country. I hate country. I want houses with windows and open doors. All the women lie in big brass beds with their babies and the men sit outside on wooden benches. Pepe el Romano is a giant. You all want him. But he'll eat you up, eat you up every one, because you're just ears of corn. No you're not. You're not even ears of corn. You're frogs without tongues!

MARTIRIO (*energetically*). Come on now, it's time for bed. (*Pushes her.*)

MARÍA JOSEFA. All right, but will you let me out afterwards?

MARTIRIO. Yes. I promise.

MARÍA JOSEFA (*crying*). My baby is a little lamb,
     I'll take him to the shore,
     I'll give him my breast and bits of ham,
     A little ant will sit at our door.

Exit. MARTIRIO *shuts the door* MARÍA JOSEFA *has gone out through and moves to the door to the yard. She hesitates, and then moves two more steps forward.*

MARTIRIO (*in a low voice*). Adela.

Pause. She goes up to the door itself.

(*Loudly.*) Adela!

ADELA *appears. Her hair is loose.*

ADELA. What do you want from me?

MARTIRIO. Leave that man!

ADELA. Who are you to tell me that?

MARTIRIO. That is no place for a woman of honour.

ADELA. Perhaps not, but you'd love to be in it.

MARTIRIO. I can't keep silent any more. This has got to end!

ADELA. This has only just begun. I've had the strength to push forward. The energy and the guts that you don't possess. I've seen death. Here, in these rooms. And now I'm leaving them to take what's mine.

MARTIRIO. He's a man without soul. And you've stolen him. He didn't come for you.

ADELA. He just came for the money, but his eyes were always fixed on me.

MARTIRIO. I won't let you have him. He must marry Angustias.

ADELA. He doesn't love her. You know that as well as I do.

MARTIRIO. Yes.

ADELA. You know that because you have seen him with me. You know he loves me.

MARTIRIO (*desperately*). Yes!

ADELA (*approaching her*). He loves me. He loves me!

MARTIRIO. Stick a knife in me if you like. I don't care. Only don't tell me that again!

ADELA. That's why you don't want him to go with me. You don't mind him kissing a woman he doesn't love, and neither do I. As far as we're concerned, he could live with Angustias for a thousand years. But you can't bear to think of him making love to me because you love him too, don't you? You love him too!

MARTIRIO. Yes, yes. Yes! I want to say it. I want to get my head clear of all these lies. I want to say it though there's so much anger inside me I feel I could explode. I want to say it. I want to say it. I love him. I love him!

ADELA (*on a sudden impulse, embracing her*). I'm sorry, Martirio, I'm sorry. But I can't help it. Don't blame me.

MARTIRIO. Don't touch me! Don't try to soften me! We're not sisters any more. We might like to be, but we can't be. Now you're just a stranger.

ADELA. There's nothing to be done. Pepe's mine. Choke on it if you like. It can't be helped. We'll go off to the banks of the river and make love amongst the reeds.

MARTIRIO. You won't!

ADELA. There is so much horror in this house. I can't bear it any more. Not now when I've tasted his kisses. Now I'll be whatever he wants me to be. Even if all the village turn against me. Even if all the village point at me, point at me with their fingers of fire and try to burn me. Even if all the so-called respectable people in this so-called respectable village pursue me and hunt me down, I'll still stand by him. Openly and without shame. And I'll gladly wear my crown of thorns.

MARTIRIO. Don't say another word!

ADELA. If you like. I'll be quiet. We'll both be. We'll go and sleep. He can marry Angustias. I don't care any more. But I'll go off to a lonely little house and live there so he can see me whenever he wants to. Whenever he needs to.

MARTIRIO. No you won't. Not while I live. Not while I've got a single drop of blood in my body!

ADELA. You can't stop me. You're just a weakling. I'll step over you. I could bring a stallion to its knees, with all the power inside me. Inside my little finger.

MARTIRIO. Don't talk so loud. Your voice annoys me. I feel so much evil inside me that's so strong it could smother me. And I can't stop it.

ADELA. They teach us to love our sisters. But that counts for nothing now. God has left me. We are both in the dark and both strangers. I look at you as if for the very first time.

We hear a whistle, and ADELA *runs to the door, but* MARTIRIO *gets in her way.*

MARTIRIO. Where are you going?

ADELA. Get away from the door!

MARTIRIO. Get past if you can!

ADELA. Get out of the way

They struggle.

MARTIRIO (*shouts*). Mother, Mother!

ADELA. Let me go!

BERNARDA *appears, in her petticoat and wearing a black shawl.*

BERNARDA. Quiet. Quiet! Why can't I kill you with the anger in my eyes? How poor I am. How feeble and weak!

MARTIRIO (*pointing to* ADELA). She was with him! Look at her petticoat all covered in straw!

BERNARDA (*turns on* ADELA). Straw is a bed for whores!

ADELA (*standing up to her*). You've no right to condemn me any more! This is when your judgements end! (*Seizes her mother's stick and breaks it.*) So much for the oppressor's stick! Don't you dare come close to me. No one has any power over me now. No one but Pepe!

Enter MAGDALENA.

MAGDALENA. Adela!

Enter LA PONCIA *and* ANGUSTIUS.

ADELA. I'm his wife now. (*To* ANGUSTIUS.) Do you understand? Understand now and tell him you understand. Go out there and tell him. He will come in here and he will command. He's as strong as a lion. Listen to him breathe.

ANGUSTIAS. Oh God!

BERNARDA. Where's my gun? (*Exit, running.*)

AMELIA *appears at the back, and looks terrified. She just pokes her head round the door.* MARTIRIO *goes out to the yard.*

ADELA (*about to leave*). None of you will have power over me!

ANGUSTIAS (*preventing her leaving*). You won't leave here. I won't let your body win! Thief! Dragging us all into the dirt!

MAGDALENA. Let her go where she wants! We'll never see her again!

A shot is fired.

BERNARDA (*coming in*). No use looking for him now.

MARTIRIO (*coming in*). That's the end of Pepe el Romano.

ADELA. Pepe! My God! Pepe! (*Exit, running.*)

LA PONCIA. Did you kill him?

MARTIRIO. No. She missed. He galloped off on his mare.

BERNARDA. My fault. Trust a woman not to shoot straight.

MAGDALENA. Then why did you lie?

MARTIRIO. To spite her! I'd like to drown her in a river of blood!

LA PONCIA. You're wicked!

MAGDALENA. Possessed by the devil!

BERNARDA. Perhaps. But it's better this way.

We hear a thud.

Adela! Adela!

LA PONCIA (*at the door*). Open the door!

BERNARDA. Open. Don't think a door can hide you from your shame.

MAID (*entering*). All the neighbours have woken up!

BERNARDA (*in a low voice, but still like a roar*). Open up, before I break down the door!

Pause. Everyone remains in total silence.

Adela!

She steps back from the door.

Break down the door!

LA PONCIA *gives the door a shove and goes in. On entering, she lets out a scream, and comes back onstage.*

What is it?

LA PONCIA (*bringing her hands up to her neck*). God give us a better death!

The DAUGHTERS *recoil violently. The* MAID *crosses herself.* BERNARDA *lets out a cry and moves to the door.*

Don't go in!

BERNARDA. No. I can't! Pepe: you're riding home, galloping through the olive groves, knowing that no one will harm you. But another day will come, and that day you will fall. Cut her down! My daughter died a virgin! Lie her on her bed and dress her in white. As a virgin! She dies a virgin! Tell the sexton to ring the funeral bell at dawn.

MARTIRIO. I envy her. She had him!

BERNARDA. No tears. Death has to be looked straight in the eye. Silence! (*To another* DAUGHTER.) I said silence! (*To another* DAUGHTER.) Save your tears for when you're alone. We'll all drown in a sea of mourning! She was the youngest daughter of Bernarda Alba and she died a virgin. Do you hear me? Silence, silence, I said! Silence!

Curtain.

The End.

19th June 1936

Translator's Note

Lorca was shot by the fascist authorities of Granada two months later. He was thirty-eight years old.